Everyday Spiritual Practice

Simple Pathways for Enriching Your Life

Edited by
Scott W. Alexander

Skinner House Books
Boston

Published by Skinner House Books, an imprint of the Unitarian
Universalist Association of Congregations, a liberal religious
organization with more than 1,000 congregations in the U.S. and
Canada. 25 Beacon Street, Boston, MA 02108-2800.

Printed in Canada.

ISBN 1-55896-375-8
978-1-55896-375-7

10 9 8 7 6 5 4
12 11 10 09

Acknowledgments

The poem "Absolutely Clear" is from *The Subject Tonight is Love:
60 Wild and Sweet Poems* by Shams-Ud-Din Muhammad Hafiz,
translated by Daniel Ladinsky. (North Myrtle Beach, SC: Pumpkin
House Press, 1996) Copyright 1996 by Daniel Ladinsky. Reprinted by
permission of Daniel Ladinsky.

Everyday spiritual practice: simple pathways for enriching your life
/ edited by Scott W. Alexander.
       p.   cm.
     Includes bibliographical references.
     ISBN 1-55896-375-8 (alk. paper)
       1. Christian life. 2. Spiritual life.   3. Spiritual formation.
4. Christian life—Unitarian Universalist authors. I. Alexander,
Scott W.
BV4501.2.E925   1999
248.4'6—dc21
                                       98-50320
                                            CIP

Contents

Introduction

It was the Greek philosopher Plato who said, "The life which is unexamined is not worth living." Many people in our culture seem caught in a rut, meandering through their days, doing only what comes easily, simply reacting to unpredictable twists and turns, failing to structure their lives in any meaningful, maturing ways.

This book offers an enriching alternative by suggesting how you can spiritually examine, shape, and care for your life—and the life around you—to achieve more wholeness, satisfaction, depth, and meaning. These suggestions range from meditation and prayer, to recycling and vegetarianism, to quilting and art. They are any activity or attitude in which you can regularly and intentionally engage, and which significantly deepens the quality of your relationship with the miracle of life both within and beyond you. This is what I call everyday spiritual practice.

While working on this collection, I was often asked, "What makes an everyday spiritual *practice* different from a casual spiritual *hobby*, something worthwhile that one simply dabbles in when one feels like it?" The answer is intentionality, regularity, and depth. Whether it is sitting zen, doing charitable giving, working with a spiritual director, or tending your relationship with loved ones, what shapes your efforts into an everyday spiritual practice is your commitment to making the activity a regular and significant part of your life.

People often associate the word "practice" with joyless discipline and unrewarding labor, like countless hours spent at a piano or computer keyboard struggling to master the skill. As I read the diverse essays in this collection, I was struck by how consistently the contributors describe the liberating, soul-satisfying pleasure their spiritual disciplines bring to their lives. Paradoxically, by choosing to embrace discipline and structure, which on the surface seems to restrict freedom and limit choice, you gain the freedom to become more fully and joyfully yourself. I hope this book will persuade you that everyday spiritual practice is not glum drudgery or puritanical labor, but rather a part of joyful, creative, and empowered living.

Our spiritual lives are often characterized by a natural ebb and flow. It is rare, though not impossible, for an individual to adopt a spiritual practice and continue it, unabated and unaltered, for a lifetime. Spiritual practices can be dropped, replaced, or restarted as circumstances change. Such flexibility and flow are natural. A spiritual practice that serves you well at this moment of your life may not serve you in the future. This book encourages you to think flexibly and freely about how your spiritual relationship with self, others, nature, and all of creation might evolve within your lifetime. Perhaps this book will become one you revisit from time to time, as your spiritual needs and circumstances shift.

Whatever your spiritual or religious affiliation, I believe you will find useful ideas in this collection. It is by no means exhaustive, but its rich diversity is a starting point for deepening your spiritual life. All the contributors to this book are clergy and laypeople from my own religious tradition, Unitarian Universalism. In our faith every individual is expected, with the help of clergy and community, to nurture and tend the garden of his or her own religious life each and every day. The open and inclusive nature of this book reflects the openness of Unitarian Universalist congregations to diverse religious paths and approaches. If you want to know more about Unitarian Universalism or the Unitarian Universalist congregation nearest you, please visit our Web site at **www.uua.org** or write the Unitarian Universalist Association of Congregations, 25 Beacon Street, Boston, MA 02108-2800.

I hope that this book will inspire, inform, and challenge you. Perhaps you will be startled to discover that you are already engaged in activities of everyday spiritual practice. Perhaps you will be challenged to deepen one or more of the existing spiritual aspects of your everyday living. Or perhaps you will be inspired to intentionally introduce one or more new spiritual practices into your life at this time. Soul-satisfying spiritual practices can be done, even amidst the demanding confusions, distractions, and duties of daily life. Enjoy reading these essays and know that you are free to live your life every day with greater mindfulness, gentleness, depth, compassion, and joy.

Scott W. Alexander

THE BASICS

Balance

Susan Manker-Seale

I want to paint the earth
in words
and sing my blessings
in the wind.

Deep in our innermost core we yearn to be connected with the mystery we call god, or nature, or the spirit. We yearn for that sense of oneness with each other and all creation, to know our place and our value. And, often, we yearn for someone to show us how to get there, to direct us to the right path that will lead us on the way to a deeper spirituality.

The problem is, finding the right path is like standing in front of a candy counter and trying to decide which piece is the right piece, the best piece. You know that it all depends on your tastes, and you need to know what you like in order to choose the best piece for you. That means that you have to have tried at least some of them to know which ones you like. Even then, it's important to acknowledge that others may find different pieces more to their liking.

There is no one right path to a deeper spirituality. There are many right paths, and the one you choose may serve for a while, and then need to be changed over time. Like the Buddha who left everything to go off in search of enlightenment, you may find yourself coming back to yourself in the end, as did he, to your own home and people, to a greater understanding of the value of the mundane alongside the spiritual, and the importance of learning to balance your life.

My daily spiritual practice is to balance. A major part of that practice involves balancing the busy, taking-for-granted moments of the day with moments to pause and appreciate what is before me in my life. I probably wouldn't even have considered this a spiritual practice, except that I've been learning to redefine the meaning of what is spiritual, and to ponder for myself what is important in my faith.

I went to a writer's workshop once in which Allen Ginsberg led us in poetry exercises. He told us to pick any word, and make combinations using it with other words. Then we were to pick the most outrageous or interesting combination and write it into a haiku. The first word I thought of was "notebook," and the silly pair I chose was "diaper notebook." This came out:

Beside the holy books
I'd like to see one
diaper notebook
well-used!

The message many of us have been given through our religious heritage is that if one wishes to be "spiritual," one must leave the worldly world. Yet the reality is that, if we have family and work, integrating a traditional spiritual practice into our daily lives is a real challenge. Try meditating with a baby in the next room!

I know there are others more disciplined than I, but I have had years when I was able to be disciplined. I used to keep a journal in early college, but rarely write that way anymore. I was taught to meditate one summer when I was out of balance in my life. For a year I meditated twice each day, to great benefit of spirit. But slowly, I let it slide, and am trying to get myself to make room for it once again. I studied aikido for a year and a half, but moved, and my new teacher didn't blend the physical with the spiritual in the way my original teacher had. I am a poet, have written poetry for most of my life, learning from the insights I discover through such a process, yet never in a regular exercise. The latest practice I engaged in was to walk for twenty minutes three times a week, for both my physical and my mental health, and I kept that up for two years until I went back to teaching full-time and the mornings I so loved were no longer open to me. I just couldn't transfer to evening, with dinner preparation and children at home. Last year I moved to Tucson, and have spent a year wondering when I would get back to walking, or would I join a Zen meditation group, or what.

Every change in my life has seemed to disrupt my pattern, and each time I've had to find out what fit my new situation. But, even though I haven't kept up these practices regularly, I have learned from them, been shaped by them. They are tools, not ends. They help us learn to slow down, to pay attention, to focus, or to empty. They are not definitions of spirituality themselves. The deep meaning of spirituality is breath. Breath is the taking in of life-giving essence from the world around us, and the release, in turn, of life-giving essence. It is a metaphor for our interdependencies: the fact that we change and are changed by our environment in a continuous play of creation. Spiritual practices are aimed at helping us understand that connectedness, to sense our oneness, to the end that our yearning is appeased in actuality. For whether you call it God/dess, Nature, Spirit, or Oneness (or some other word), the feeling of presence is very real for many of us. It is a feeling which sustains me, and fills me with appreciation for all that is my life.

We can practice spirituality in our daily lives, in our daily activities, by remembering to pause, pay attention, and feel appreciation for what is before us. Paying attention means using all of our senses in being in the world and in the moment. Stop a moment. Feel the chair in which you are sitting. Notice the temperature around you. Listen for the sounds of your background symphony. Breathe. Appreciate the colors of your clothes, your skin, the sky, or the ceiling. Focus on appreciating the peace out of which you have found the time to read or listen to these words. Remember the feeling of oneness with creation, and try to bring that back into being. This practice only takes a few moments and is not bound by place or time or ritual.

Once, as I paused in writing at my desk to listen, I heard, and wrote a poem:

Poem for Thursday

Dove calls through busy morning walls
The dove calls
She calls
And silence fills my mind
Hush!
The dove calls.

Out of our busyness, we are called back into balance, back into ourselves and the silence of present being. But it is not just back into ourselves to which we are called; it is also to the awareness of the continuous presence of the environment around us and within us. We are called to remember our relationships and our dependencies. We are called to once again feel the oneness which sustains our being in balance with creation, and to do so with wonder and appreciation.

There is nothing difficult about this practice. There are times, I will admit, when it is harder to recall that sense of presence and connection. When that happens, I usually realize that I've gotten somewhat out of touch with my body, and so I spend a little more time putting myself behind my eyes, so to speak. I don't just see; I see broadly, to the edges of my sockets, my brows and lashes. I put myself back into my hands and arms, feel my feet and the length of my body. I find my heartbeat, and my breath. As I become aware once again of the vessel which is me, the sense of awareness of presence grows, expands into the space around me, connecting me to all that I see and hear and touch and feel and taste. Balance returns.

We live our lives too much in a shell built of inattention and distraction. An analogy is the shoes we wear that keep us from feeling the ground. A few years ago my family went up to Sedona to play and hike among the rocks. The path was finely ground red dirt, the kind that puffs as you walk on it. My children begged to take their shoes off. At first, all I could think of were such practical worries as hidden glass, or snakes, or stubbed toes. Thank goodness they were persistent. The truth was that we needed to take off our shoes; we needed to feel the earth beneath our skin. I will never forget that cool, incredibly soft Sedona dirt molding itself to every footprint. Too bad for the strange glances of passing hikers. We had a wonderful time.

The world is full of wonder, if we but stop and pay attention. It is there, waiting to feed us, even in very difficult situations. The day is made up of moments, and each moment can be an eternity of peace to those experiencing pain or grief. They are like blessings, and we count them, one by one throughout the day. They help us keep our balance.

Pause for those moments every so often to listen and to look, to feel and to smell, to taste and to appreciate, to feel thankful for the beauty which is around us even in the smallest grains of red dirt and in the grandest blue of sky. The mundane world is a source of deep spirituality. Notice it, appreciate it, for you are it and it is you. This spiritual practice is one tool to help us feel our connectedness and sense the oneness for which we yearn.

Like hungry swallows
we search
for there is emptiness
in every breast.

We do not have to fit ourselves to someone's prescribed discipline in order to feel we are being spiritual. Spirituality is with us always, and our individual situations will define the tools we choose to use, if we take the time to listen to ourselves and know our joys and yearnings, whether for quiet or a walk in beauty, for exercise or music, for sunsets or sunrises, for strenuous activity or the hand in ours, for the glance of a child, for effort or work that is meaningful, for the creative task or the work of community, or for the moments of appreciation which are available to us anytime and anywhere. Whichever path you choose, may you find that for which you search, and your yearning be fulfilled.

Listening to Our Lives

Kathleen McTigue

It's easy to develop an attitude problem when it comes to the question of spiritual discipline, especially for those of us leading lives characterized by relentlessly overladen days. Through most of my life I've understood the notion of spiritual discipline with the emphasis on the word *discipline*. It was something to strive for, an ideal with mingled connotations of asceticism and serenity regardless of the particular practice that might be chosen.

Over the years I settled mostly on the common disciplines of prayer and silent meditation, depending on whether the primordial Catholic or the more recent Buddhist strains of my theology were dominant. For many years my struggle was mostly with what seemed to be my own lack of discipline: I'd procrastinate or get distracted or lazy, and would have to coax myself back into silence and contemplation. During certain stretches of time I could settle into the rhythm I wanted, with prayer and meditation a clear and settled part of my daily routine. Inevitably, though, some sort of distraction would prevail and I'd be wrestling with myself again, frustrated at what I labeled a lack of discipline.

On the fateful day in my mid-thirties when my first child was born, discipline became the least of my problems. How in the world can any of us manage a spiritual practice when our days are spent chaotically juggling work and family? On some days mere survival—without murdering spouse, children, or pets—seems downright miraculous.

There is an old folk tale from the Christian tradition about the saintly Brother Bruno, who was at prayer one night when he found his concentration interrupted by the loud croaking of a bullfrog. He kept trying to ignore the noise, but the harder he tried to concentrate the more annoying the sound became. Finally he leaned out of his window and shouted, "Quiet! I'm at my prayers!" Instantly there was complete silence, as the bullfrog and every other creature obeyed his command. Brother Bruno settled back into prayer, but now he found himself even more deeply disturbed by a nagging doubt: Why would God create the bullfrog and its rasping voice unless there was something pleasing in the sound? Could it be that Bruno's own prayer sounded, to God's ears, like the arrogant croaking of another sort of frog?

Bruno could not push away this uneasiness, and so he finally leaned out his window again and gave the command, "Sing!" The throaty croak of the bullfrog again filled the air, along with all the other creatures that had fallen silent. Brother Bruno listened carefully to the sound, and to his amazement he discovered that it was beautiful. Once he no longer resisted it as noise, the joyful concert actually enriched the peacefulness of the night. With that discovery, Bruno understood for the first time in his life what it really meant to pray.

Ancient though it is, this story is an excellent illustration of the modern therapeutic term "reframing." To reframe a problem or issue means exactly that: We recognize that what we're contemplating is shaped by the perspective or "frame" we're used to, and we try a different frame or angle in order to see the problem differently. When reframing works well, it can even make a problem disappear: It changes our perspective so radically that what once troubled us just doesn't seem to matter anymore. That's what happened to Brother Bruno in the story: His irritable quest for silence was resolved by a changed frame. In that new frame, the croaking frog was no longer an interruption, and the changed perspective even heralded a new level of enlightenment. In the moment of finally listening to the language of the world around him, Brother Bruno learned for the first time in his life what it really meant to pray. When he let go of his quest for silence, he found a deeper prayer in the noise of the world around him.

When I first heard this story I found myself feeling just a wee bit smug about the fact that I already love the music of the frogs and the crickets and the myriad voices that float in my window during the summer. I can't recall ever being in Brother Bruno's place, wishing the world would hush so that my glorious and important prayer could rise up to God's waiting ears. But my smugness evaporated as I pictured the scene recounted in the story, the devout Bruno settling into his hours of prayer. How long had it been since I'd even attempted that kind of concentrated prayer?

Brother Bruno was leading the monastic life, in which prayer at night and at all hours of the day was at the heart of his routine. The whole point of the monastic life is to frame our world so that prayerfulness lies at the very center of the frame. In many ways the image we hold of the monastic life characterizes our beliefs about what it means to walk a serious religious path, regardless of our theologies or religious backgrounds. Every faith has its ascetics and its saints, and with rare exceptions they are the ones who followed a monastic path, separating themselves from the normal flow of life in our world in order to dedicate themselves with a single-minded focus on their quest for spiritual depth.

Many of us who can't claim to be either saints or ascetics nevertheless go on retreat from time to time in contemplative or monastic settings; sometimes those retreats may even be for long periods of time. But very few of us will truly enter the monastic life and adopt a pattern to our days in which the attentive listening of spiritual discipline lies at the center of all we do. As long as our vision of spiritual growth is restricted to such rigorous discipline, the only conclusion is that those of us who live immersed in the day-to-day world are not as serious as we might be about our spiritual lives.

Perhaps growth will come to us in ragged little fragments we snatch as we race by, but if it depends on long, focused periods of silence, we're out of luck.

For many of us, our lives are framed with frenetic rather than measured edges. We catapult into each morning, driven out of too little sleep by the alarm clock or the first stirrings of children. We grope our way to the coffee and the shower, get ourselves and sundry children out the door and into our respective currents of the day, and respond to the crises and the routine demands we meet. We come home and the time is still filled and more than filled with the various duties that keep our domestic hearths burning. When the children are asleep and the chores are finished, some of us finally have time to slow down and find the quiet to listen to our lives— as long as we don't mind nodding off to sleep as we do it.

I recently learned that a colleague of mine begins every day with up to an hour of meditation and yoga. A newspaper article about her began with a photo of her lying on a mat in a yoga position, the clean lines of her hardwood floor stretching out on either side and giving a sense of visual calmness and order along with the calmness and order implied by her discipline.

This is not a snapshot of my life. In fact the longer I looked at the picture and tried to project myself into it, the more amusing it started to look to me. Because if the photo had been of me, I would have been surrounded by a monstrous clutter of toys, overdue library books, unwashed laundry, children's crayons and drawings, and dirty dishes. There would have to be at least one child crying in the background or yelling at a sibling, and a cat nudging my face to be fed. And I, of course, would not be lying there in meditation, profound or otherwise, but would be snoring.

To admit this to myself is to invite a stab of envy, if not for the meditative discipline itself, then at least for the clean and pristine room! But since envy brings me no closer to deepening my own spiritual life, I find myself wondering instead whether it might be time for some reframing. Remembering the lesson Brother Bruno learned, I ask: Since my spiritual life is not framed by silence and contemplation, where can I find that life within the noise and activity that surround me? How can I find the moment that came to Brother Bruno, the moment in which, by really listening to the language of my world, I discover the deeper and truer prayer?

Author Kathleen Norris writes of the most significant thing she learned from her months with the Benedictines: "Gradually my perspective on time . . . changed. In our culture, time can seem like an enemy: It chews us up and spits us out with appalling ease. But the monastic perspective welcomes time as a gift from God and seeks to put it to good use rather than allowing us to be used up by it . . . . Liturgical time is essentially poetic time, oriented toward process rather than productivity."

What does it mean to see our lives in a frame oriented toward process rather than productivity? Every spiritual discipline is designed to help us listen more deeply to our lives. If the recognizable disciplines such as prayer and meditation are sporadic and fleeting at best, then is there some other way to grab hold of what they try to teach us? In other words, is there a way for us to hear not the muddle of voices that keeps us from our prayer, but the prayer within even that muddle of voices?

I don't lose sight of the need and the hope for a more concentrated prayer life and more quiet, meditative time, but in its absence I have discovered a short and simple practice at night in the brief, peaceful moments between turning out the light and falling asleep. It's a practice that inevitably helps me listen more deeply to the life I really lead, to avoid the trap of longing for some illusory growth that might come in the contemplative life I have not chosen.

My spiritual practice consists of this: I think back on the events of the day and ask the question, "Where was God in this day?" It's a question that can be asked in a dozen different theological voices, and if God language fails to resonate, then we might ask merely, "Where today did I really hear the language of my life?" The question puts a sheen of attentiveness and care on even the most mundane dimensions of the day. It gives us a way to cradle the moments of a day just lived and see them again before they're too far away, to notice the regrets and failings as well as the joys.

Then we see that even lacking the contemplative silence, the voice of our lives that we need to hear is whispering. I find it in my child's question or in the walk that I squeezed in at twilight; it was there when the sales clerk suddenly spoke with tears about her husband's death and there when I tasted the sweetness of a perfect pear and ate it slowly, carefully, paying attention. It's there in the work done well and with pleasure and also there in the lessons learned in failings, large and small.

This simple query has a long reach, and it accomplishes much more than a retrospective look. To fall asleep with the question "Where in this day did I really hear the language of my life?" moves us every day a little nearer to awakening with the question "Where today will I really hear the language of my life?" Where today will I find God? The calm eye of attention, the deeper wisdom of mindfulness, begin to seep in, as they do with any spiritual discipline faithfully practiced.

For many of us, our daily prayer will never arise out of silence, but from the thrumming heart of things right where we live. So it will be there, at the heart that never stops beating, that we can most clearly listen to our lives and discern the path that is ours to walk.

The Middle Way

Michael A. Schuler

Most people know the legend: how Siddhartha, desperate for an answer to the riddle of existence, traded a life of comfort and ease for one of austerity and complete self-denial. Like many of his Hindu contemporaries, Siddhartha believed that by cudgeling his body into submission he could kill desire, expand his consciousness, and cancel the influence of karma. But years of superhuman exertion left the young seeker gravely weakened and no closer to enlightenment. Finally, Siddhartha adopted a more sensible, moderate approach to spiritual practice, and before long achieved his purpose while meditating under the Bo tree. He discovered the principle of the "middle way," which Buddhism continues to teach to this day.

The middle way is a comprehensive approach to being in the world, and it is the path I have chosen. It has a place in other religious traditions as well. Balance, harmony, and equilibrium are concepts critical to Taoism and occupy a central place in the teachings of the *Tao Te Ching*. Horace and his successors among the Stoics offered the concept of "temperance" as a Western complement to the middle way. In Christianity, several gospel accounts show Jesus practicing and advocating sensible moderation. If one was hungry, gathering food on the Sabbath was justifiable. Invited to a wedding, one ate and drank like the other guests. His more abstemious compatriots accused him of gluttony, but Jesus' common-sense approach called a spirituality controlled by rigid legal strictures into question.

Walking the middle way means bringing a certain attitude and awareness to the everyday business of living. It is "spiritual practice" in the fullest sense because it involves the recognition that everything a person does has spiritual ramifications; everything factors into one's spiritual fulfillment. But the middle way best serves as a guiding principle, not as an inviolable rule. Paradoxically, if we are too scrupulous, the middle way can become just another obsession— a distraction and a diversion from the greater task.

The middle way offers a useful approach to some of the everyday issues of modern American life. With regard to food, for example, practicing the middle way means thinking about what I eat and making choices that are consistent with my values and that keep me feeling fit and healthy. Above all, I want to keep enough flexibility in my diet that when situations arise (and they often do) when the foods I prefer aren't readily available, I won't find myself becoming upset, angry, disappointed, or depressed. I refuse to agonize over my diet. "It isn't what goes into our mouths that defiles us," Jesus said, "but what comes out of our mouths that is defiling." Our eventual goal should be to develop a comfortable relationship with food in general.

For many people, exercise is as difficult to deal with as food. When we exercise too much, we may become tired, impatient, and irritable, hindering our work, relationships, and spiritual goals. When we exercise too little, we become less healthy physically and mentally, and we lessen our ability to participate in the many schools of spiritual practice that make stretching, walking, running, and physical chores part of the daily discipline. Each physical self is different, and "body disciplines" need to be individually tailored. But the middle way requires that we attend to this element of spiritual practice. The spirit and body are connected. The awakening of our so-called higher self requires that the carnal also be given its due.

Time management is another issue that the middle way can help us to approach. Americans are probably as over-

worked and overstimulated as any people in history; non-
natives often remark upon the furious pace of American life.
But the cost to the human spirit is high. We don't know how to
sit still; we don't know what to do with ourselves when the
TV's on the fritz, the mall closes, or Social Security kicks in.

Following the middle way, I have learned to live comfortably *within* myself by spending time each day, each week,
every year by myself. When our collective work and social
life is complemented by periods of solitude, we are walking
in the middle way. We need, every day, to reserve a short
period of time to be alone—away from books, radios, tele-
phones, computers, pets, as well as other people. We can sit
quietly and meditate, write in a journal, take a long walk,
or do whatever we need to relax, heal, and review recent life
events. One day a week the same pattern is repeated, but for
a longer period; the important thing, as the ancients recognized, is to "observe a Sabbath and keep it holy." A yearly
retreat is also desirable. Members of Buddhist communities
or "sanghas" might spend an entire month in withdrawal.
This is not vacation, which for Americans typically involves
even more work and worry than usual. A retreat is true down
time, an engraved invitation to the spirit to emerge, express
itself, and grow.

The competing demands of everyday life also require ethi-
cal reflection and practice. Wrestling with issues of right and
wrong, harming and non-harming, serving self or serving
others, often leaves us feeling frustrated and bewildered.
What does responsibility mean? How do I become a boon
rather than a burden to the world? Here, too, the middle
way can help. In Buddhist thinking, two important principles
exist in dynamic tension: compassion and impermanence. It
is our duty and our destiny to lead loving lives. But all the
love in the world will not change the fact that things pass
away; every particle of creation is subject to the law of impermanence. To walk in the middle way, then, means loving
and honoring the world while learning to temper our grief
with acceptance.

Following the middle way isn't easy. Most people are pretty inconsistent and unsteady about managing their own lives. We settle upon a goal, develop an appropriate strategy, and for several weeks or months pursue our aim with considerable energy and diligence. But then our resolve begins to falter, our efforts slacken, old habits reassert themselves, and pretty soon we are right back where we started. A year later we may convince ourselves to try again, and the cycle repeats itself. Eating and drinking sensibly, staying moderately active, reserving time regularly for friends and family, maintaining an active prayer life, and reconnecting daily with the energies of Nature are disciplines we do not perform well. Rather, we eat either a lot of food or none, catch up on sleep rather than awaken each morning feeling rested, overwork ourselves at the gym one day and cope with sore muscles the rest of the week. Ours is a feast-or-famine mentality, swinging wildly (and often miserably) between self-indulgence and self-denial. It takes considerable discipline to live according to the middle way.

My recent experience in a tai chi program made this principle clear to me all over again. Two years ago I started the program, determined to master the basic form and add this venerable Eastern exercise to my spiritual toolbox. I intended not just to acquire its calming effects and physiological benefits but to master the entire, complicated form and to make it integral to my spiritual development. Accordingly, I enrolled at a well-regarded academy devoted exclusively to the "soft" martial arts, and paid upfront for an entire year of classes.

Tai chi is one of those exercises that looks deceptively simple to casual observers but is amazingly difficult to master. It requires a year and a half of weekly classes and daily practice at home to learn the rudiments of a Taiwanese variation on the Yang-style short form I was taught. It will take at least another year before I know the form well enough to do it without hitches or miscues. My teachers say that a lifetime isn't too long to polish one's tai chi technique.

Approximately two dozen men and women enrolled in the beginner-level class I first attended. Yet only about four of us completed the entire process. Despite the patience and capability of our instructors, most of the students dropped out a third or halfway through. This observation highlights the main problem most people have with the middle way. Tai chi isn't a terribly demanding practice. Unusual strength and dexterity aren't required to execute the basic form. It is a good, moderate, "mindful" form of exercise which, according to traditional Chinese teachings, replenishes the body's subtle energies. All tai chi really demands is diligence.

I know of no shortcuts, no alternative curriculum. Achievement in spirituality—as in science, athletics, or the arts—requires clear focus and steady application. Zen master Thich Nhat Hanh makes the point much more eloquently when he says, "The miracle is not to walk on water. The miracle is to walk on the green earth in the present moment, to appreciate the peace and beauty that are available now. It is not a matter of faith; it is a matter of practice."

I continue to practice, trying to figure out how to make the best use of the middle way, resolving to make it my way in good humor and with a degree of grace.

Eclectic Spirituality

Barbara Wells

I grew up a preacher's kid. From very early on, I loved the life of the church; the supportive community, the endlessly interesting and stimulating spiritual elements. In the 1960s and 1970s, when I was growing up, words like "spiritual practice" and "devotional life" weren't used in the liberal church. Yet even without the words, I was being trained in the practice of spirituality.

I have come to realize that my spiritual practice can best be described as "eclectic." I have been fed through diverse and what may seem to be conflicting ways. I have gained spiritual knowledge in places as different as a college classroom and a New Age support group. I have journaled, prayed, meditated, danced, and sung to nurture my spirit. I have worshipped alone on a mountainside and in a ballroom filled with thousands. I have gone months without doing anything that looks remotely spiritual and have prayed every day for weeks at a time. That variety has been extraordinarily fulfilling and good for my soul.

Eclectic spiritual practice goes against the prevailing view that spiritual practice is like exercise: It must be a consistent, daily regimen, or your spirit will wither and die. Because this belief is so common, I have on occasion been called to task for not being "spiritual enough." But I believe there is no one-size-fits-all spirituality. Each person's spiritual practice will look different from everyone else's. For many, the ideal is a regular practice that springs from one tradition and follows one path. But for others, broader boundaries along which to explore our spirits are what we need. If you fall into this latter category, a few things I've learned along the way may be of help.

While my spiritual practice has embraced various sources and forms of expression, it has consistently involved three primary elements: personal devotion, finding a mentor, and worshipping in community. Each of these has been important to me, both as a person and as a religious leader. At times, one seems more important than the other. Over time, they have all emerged as essential elements for giving deeper meaning and joy to my soul. These three elements are as old as religion itself, yet they are fresh and alive to me.

Personal devotion is simply that—personal. Depending on your religious background and inclinations, you will likely find some practices that provide you with the reflection necessary to deepen your sense of yourself and your place in this world. For me, journaling has been one key element. I have written in a journal of one kind or another since I was ten years old. At other times, I use an altar and pray in the Wiccan fashion, listen to music and let my heart wander where it will, or use poetry or the powerful words of religious writers to stimulate my spirit. As long as the practice gives me the space to be who I am and where I am at that moment, it works.

While personal reflective space is essential, our spiritual lives are not meant to be lived alone. Much of the literature on spiritual practice seems to assume an introverted nature. Yet extroverts are spiritual, too! I have found a need throughout my life for companionship on the journey. Spiritual mentors are a great way to get support and guidance. My religious mentors have ranged from a nurse/counselor who, through her use of guided imagery, awakened in me a depth I had never explored before, to a Wiccan priestess, who, in the privacy of my living room, teaches me chants and helps me to get in touch with the power inherent in all of life. At certain way stations in my life, I have sought out teachers and they have been there. I encourage you to do the same.

Finally, my spiritual practice includes regular, communal worship. For me, worship has always been an essential part of life. (I am lucky in that I am able to worship while leading services. I know that can be hard for some professional religious leaders to do.) For me, worshipping regularly is a way to remember who I am, who my people are, what my tradition demands. I love to be in a church, yet I also am happy to worship communally at retreat centers, conferences, clergy gatherings, interfaith events. The act of coming together to celebrate life and reflect on its paradoxes and challenges deeply nurtures my being. While I might go a month without attending church, I start to feel anxious if it lasts any longer than that. Worshipping in community is a going home for my spirit and I never want to do without it.

Eclectic spiritual practice is not easy. Without a set discipline to follow, it requires willingness to explore many options and find what will work best. Some paths I have trod have proven to be dead ends. Others taught me a lot but were left behind as I changed and grew. At times, I have found the openness challenging.

Yet, this flexibility does provide the freedom to focus more on a particular aspect of my eclectic spiritual path at any given time. For example, during the time I was working with a New Age Christian teacher, much of my personal spiritual practice reflected her bias. As I discovered that some of the readings and other avenues for spiritual practice didn't reach me, I stopped doing them, even though I continued my work with her. I found that I had to trust my own instincts even as I valued her teaching.

I've also had the freedom to put much of my spiritual practice on hold at certain times. This usually occurs when I'm on vacation or in another beautiful natural setting. Perhaps during these times the spirit of God is very close and doesn't require formal settings or practices to be reached. Whatever the reason, after these brief interludes I usually return to my practice none the worse for wear.

At other times, I've pursued spiritual practice much more vigorously. It is most necessary, I have found, when I am too busy to have time for it. At one particular time, when everything seemed to be falling apart around me and I had very little time to deal with anything, I found myself even more compelled to do regular personal reflection, meet weekly with my teacher, and worship with my community. Doing so enabled me to weather one of the most difficult periods in my life.

Comfort and spiritual peaks are wonderful, but spiritual practice is ultimately designed for something more: to make us better people and to bring our gifts into the world. The most important spiritual task we have as human beings is to make this planet kinder, more humane, and more just. My eclectic spiritual practice works for me because it helps me stay centered on who I am, why I'm here, and what I am to do. I believe I am a better person because of the unique path I have chosen.

If you want to practice eclectic spirituality, simply start walking on your own individual path. Find something you enjoy doing—perhaps one of the practices described in this book—that allows you to reflect on your life and to open yourself to all that is holy. Look for a teacher you trust, perhaps a counselor, minister, or fellow church member who has wisdom to share. Get yourself to a religious community and throw yourself into its worship life. Be there whenever you can, and strive to let it nurture you even as it challenges you.

This eclectic path has worked for me. May you find joy as you move along your own unique spiritual journey.

A Spiritual Maintenance Schedule

Arvid Straube

Most of us spend no time on spiritual maintenance at all. This doesn't mean that we don't have a spiritual life. Grace does happen. The spirit will break in to our obsessed, anxious lives on occasion, whether we do anything about it or not. But we can derive immeasurable benefit from spending just a little bit of time each day nurturing our spiritual life. The benefits are feeling more calm, a feeling of being more available to oneself and to other people, of being more loving, of being in touch with a joy that does not depend on whether our outward circumstances are happy or not. It means getting in touch more often with the deep currents and purposes of our lives.

At the end of this chapter you will find a schedule for spiritual maintenance. It's like the schedule you have in the owner's manual for your automobile. How often do you change the oil? How often do you get a tune-up? How often do you check your tires? I tried to make it simple. Realize that in keeping this schedule simple I have idealized it to the point where it might not fit some of you, but at least it's a starting point in reflecting how your lives might improve by paying attention to the spirit.

For many, the first item on that schedule is the most important: daily practice, just spending as few as ten minutes a day—ideally thirty—in prayer or meditation or silent reflection. I believe that no matter how busy you are, if you really want to, anyone can find fifteen minutes some time in the day for this purpose.

First let's consider prayer. Prayer is a topic that's made much too complicated by all the books and teachings on it. The fact is that prayer is the most simple, natural thing in the world. The only problem with prayer is to take away all the attitudes and preconceptions that keep us from prayer. I've come to think that prayer is simply being in touch with the most honest, deepest desires of the heart. What we have to push aside, then, are ideas about how we should feel, what we should want. What we need to push aside are ideas we learned about what kinds of words or language we should use, or even the idea that we need to use any kind of language at all. What we need to push aside is the idea that we need to have a systematic theology all worked out about the nature of God, the universe, human purpose, before we are qualified to turn our hearts in prayer. We don't need to have a definition of ultimate reality to pray. There's no specific idea of God that's necessary. Prayer is simply getting in touch with the deepest desires and currents of the heart in quiet, and in as much trust as we can muster, with as much honesty as we can possibly find. That's all. Prayers pray themselves. As Paul says in his letter to the Romans, "We cannot pray as we ought, but the spirit prays for us in groans too deep for words."

Meditation, I think, by my definition, is a form of prayer, even though it doesn't refer to any deity in particular. It's easy to learn. It's not easy to do, but it's easy to learn. You don't even have to be able to sit still. In fact, some forms of meditation involve movement, like walking meditation and yoga. They're all effective; they can make a big difference in your spiritual health, and we're finding more and more evidence that prayer and meditation have a tremendous impact on our physical health as well. They help us find our wholeness. There are so many ways to meditate. If a technique or particular practice does not appeal to you, remember that there are hundreds of others. One of them will appeal to you and help your heart find its way on the path.

The second item on the list comes from an ancient admonition from the Torah, "Remember the Sabbath Day and keep it holy." This too is much simpler than it's been made out to be by some religious teachers. All it means is that you take one day in the week where you don't do anything that you're obligated to do. This is a religious practice—you don't do anything that you're obligated to do. You don't work or shop. You just enjoy being alive. I think Wordsworth put his finger on the pulse of our time when he said, "Getting and spending, we lay waste our powers." And we do! We're spending most of our time either earning, spending what we've earned, or maintaining what we've bought. We don't even really have time to enjoy what we've bought, sometimes, because we're so busy getting, buying, and maintaining. We keep the Sabbath by picking one day a week—it doesn't have to be Sunday—of no working and no chores, no shopping and no maintenance. It's a time to rest, to enjoy family, friends, and loved ones. It's a time for reflection, a time for reading, for good food, playing, praying, and lovemaking. For families with children, I think this is the most important item on the list, because we are raising a generation of children who don't have their parents' time. When I've preached about the Sabbath, parents come to me and say, "It's just not possible. There are all the chores that have been saved up." Maybe it's not possible, for you. But what's more important? Time with your children or things for your children? Look honestly, and think about whether there might be a way to simplify life, so that at least for twenty-four hours a week you can be with your family and your partner with no obligations in the way.

The next item on the list is, at least monthly, being part of a group that nurtures your spiritual development. For many people, these are twelve-step groups like Alcoholics Anonymous. One of the reasons I think that twelve-step groups have proliferated—so that we now have Gamblers Anonymous, Overeaters Anonymous, Shoppers Anonymous, Sexaholics Anonymous—is that what these groups do is provide a spiritual program and the support for that spiritual program. They really help people with their daily spiritual practice. In fact, Bernie Siegal goes so far as to say that you should fake a problem if you don't have one. I'm not so sure about that. The fact is that all of us are addicted to something, so you might find a group that you can legitimately be a part of. If it's not a twelve-step group, it certainly could be a men's group or a women's group, or a prayer group, or a meditation group, or a dream group—any group that meets with the purpose of encouraging each other in our spiritual growth and helping each other to see where the spirit might be leading us now. The possible format and structure of these groups is endless. I believe that one of the most important missions of any religious congregation is to provide as wide a variety of these groups as is practical.

Yearly, I recommend, if it's at all possible, a three- to ten-day guided retreat. This is a retreat guided by someone who is familiar with the particular discipline or path that you're following: meditation or prayer. If you are working with a teacher, perhaps he or she offers such a retreat. Keep your eyes open for recommendations for retreat centers in your area. The book *Silence, Simplicity, Solitude* by David Cooper is a wonderful book about retreats that gives more information about retreat centers and teachers. It helps to talk with students of particular teachers before making such an important time and spirit commitment.

I really hesitated for a long time offering this schedule, because I was worried that I would help to foster a misconception. I don't want you to think that the things on the schedule are spiritual and the rest of our lives are not. The goal of these practices is to help us get to the point where our whole lives are spiritual practice. There is no difference between prayer and the living of life. There is no difference between meditation and the living of life. The goal is to make our whole lives spiritual. Here there's an important concept, and that is mindfulness of the present moment. Most meditation techniques say come back to something in the present moment: our breath, a candle flame, a word or sentence. Anything we are doing can be a mantra. We can pay attention to our walking when we walk; we can pay attention to our eating when we eat; we can pay attention with all of our being to our working when we work, to our conversation when we speak. We can't always do this, but, as Sogyal Rimpoche, author of *The Tibetan Book of Living and Dying,* says so wonderfully, we can remember to remember, when we remember. We can always bring our attention back to the present moment, maybe with little mindfulness bells. In Thich Nhat Hanh's meditation retreats, there's always a bell going off. When the bell goes off, you stop whatever you're doing and take three mindful breaths. So put bells all around your life, take three mindful breaths when you get behind the wheel of a car, do some mindful walking as you walk from your car to your workplace. Put these little moments of mindfulness into your life.

Since we can't always be mindful, there are precepts to help us. Precepts are behaviors that you have committed yourself to in your best moments, that will remind you to stick with your highest resolves when you're vulnerable and in your worst moments. All great religions have precepts. You know about the Ten Commandments. Well, the Buddhist Five Precepts are like this:

- Don't kill any living being.
- Don't take what is not offered to you.
- Be honest and faithful to your commitments in sexual behavior.
- Speak honestly and kindly.
- Don't use alcohol or other drugs to the point of dulling your perception or judgment.

Think about what standards of behavior you would like to hold yourself to. Write them down. Know what they are so that in moments when you are more vulnerable and less mindful, you'll remember the moments of your high resolve.

When I was at a retreat with Thich Nhat Hanh, he read a question from one of the participants. The man said, "I've learned all these wonderful spiritual practices, but I have a life, I have a job, I have a family. I'm too busy to do these. How can I live a spiritual life?" Thich Nhat Hanh said it doesn't take any time at all to be mindful of the present moment. It's simply remembering to come back. It's simply committing oneself to the precepts: trying to behave impeccably, knowing that one never can reach that height of impeccable behavior, but holding it up like the North Star and following it, not to reach the star, but to know that one has come much farther in a northerly direction. It's all about remembering to treat ourselves and others with mindfulness and care and love and respect.

Maintaining our spiritual lives is not a hard thing to do. I wish you luck and resolve in your spiritual journey.

A SPIRITUAL MAINTENANCE SCHEDULE

Once a day
Spend ten to thirty minutes in prayer and/or meditation

Once a week
Take a day free of obligations or work to rest: reflect; enjoy loved ones, family, and friends; enjoy good food, love-making, reading, praying . . . whatever renews and fulfills you. "Remember the Sabbath Day and keep it holy."

At least monthly
Meet with a group that nurtures your spiritual development—men's or women's group, meditation group, twelve-step group.

At least yearly
Take a three- to ten-day guided retreat away from home at a Christian retreat center, meditation retreat, yoga camp, or personal growth center.

For more information about ritual, see Robert Fulghum's *From Beginning to End.*

ENGAGING THE MIND

Contemplation

Silent Retreats

Andrew C. Kennedy

"You're going to do *what*?" my brother asked.

"I'm going on a silent retreat for the weekend," I reiterated. After a pause, he replied. "Why in the world would you want to do *that*?"

My brother's reaction to the idea of a weekend—let alone a week or a month—of silence was understandable, but silent retreats have a long history among many different spiritual traditions. From Jesus' forty days in the desert to Mohammed's cave retreats on Mount Hara outside of Mecca, from the Buddha's annual retreats during the rainy season to the Native American sojourns in the wilderness, voluntarily remaining silent, alone and in groups, is an ancient spiritual practice.

Still, it is a fair question: Why bother to set aside time for silence today? Let me answer this question, in part, with a story. There once was a rabbi whose custom it was to pray for an hour each morning. The rabbi was asked, "But what about when you're busy? Do you cut back to a half-hour or fifteen minutes?" "Oh, no," the rabbi replied. "When I'm really busy, then I pray for two hours."

Indeed, it is when we are busiest that we most need to keep in mind the big picture of our lives, so that we are able to appropriately and wisely prioritize among the many competing commitments for our time. As a practical matter, setting aside time for silence can help us to do that, helping us to maintain a healthy balance among the myriad activities that make up our lives.

In addition to its practical benefits, going into silence for a weekend or a week can also be a deeply spiritual experience. Silence is irreducibly elemental. It is as basic as the air we breathe and the water we drink. It is as fundamental as love, life, and death, yet it is rarely expressly sought, explored, or discussed. We cannot see, taste, touch, or smell it. We can only hear it by its absence. Yet the reality of silence cannot be doubted.

Moreover, as contemporary Swiss philosopher Max Picard notes in his book *The World of Silence,* silence is not just the absence of sound. Rather, it is, Picard suggests, "a primary, objective reality, which cannot be traced back to anything else. It cannot be replaced by anything else; it cannot be exchanged for anything else." Silence just is. And as obvious, ever-present, and unobtrusive as it is, it is also an elemental, multifaceted, and deeply spiritual reality. It preceded the big bang and will remain long after the last quark disintegrates. Thus, not only because of the practical aspects of helping us to reestablish our priorities but also because of its deep, elemental, spiritual aspects, silence is eminently worthy of our attention.

Silent meditation or prayer is the most common spiritual discipline centered around silence. Silent retreats, on the other hand, are not as widely appreciated.

What do you do on a silent retreat? Whatever you need to do to care for yourself, to get in touch with the deeper issues of your life and attend to them. If you are not sure what needs attention in your life, then you may need to begin simply by stopping for a while in order to listen to your body, to your soul, to the voice of your inner wisdom. They will guide you to what you need to do to care for yourself. (In some silent retreat settings, a spiritual director may meet with you periodically to help you discern your needs.)

If you find you need to simply relax and unwind (which many people do, especially those of us who are chronically busy, and especially toward the beginning of a retreat), then do it: Relax and unwind. Walk in the woods, wander, sit in the sun, take a nap. But try to minimize or refrain from reading; reading is verbal and focused and can lead away from reflection and unprogrammed relaxing.

If you find you have an important personal or professional decision to make or an intimate relationship to repair or reassess, then take the time on long, leisurely walks or sitting in a comfortable chair to ponder your situation and your options.

If you find you need to grieve an unresolved loss, then a silent retreat provides a wonderful opportunity to grieve. It may even be a loss from many years ago that you never had the "time" or the "space" to fully experience. It is never too late to grieve. Mourning is healing, and it ultimately helps you to uncover your joy.

Dante, in his *Divine Comedy*, once wrote, "In the middle of the road of my life, I awoke in a dark wood where the true way was wholly lost." At such times, we may find ourselves lost in the midst of deep pain and confusion, dead ends and dark woods. While silent retreats are no substitute for therapy and no panacea for life's problems, they can be an excellent way to step back from daily demands and distractions, regain perspective, and reassess where we are and where we might go next on the journey of our lives.

Another thing to do on a silent retreat is to take a systematic inventory of your life. One tool I have developed to assist myself in this regard is to examine five basic areas, or relationships, in my life, that, when taken together, encompass nearly the whole of my life. The five relationships, beginning with myself and moving outwards in five concentric circles of concern, include myself, others, the world, nature, and the cosmos. For each of these areas, there is an ancient imperative to consider.

First I examine my relationship to myself. I ask, Who am I? Father, husband, brother, friend, colleague, soccer player, etc. What are my issues? What are the key sources of my self-esteem, my joy, my pain? What am I—or should I be—working on within myself? How might I be deceiving myself? For what am I living, and for what would I die? The ancient imperative, here attributed to Socrates (and others) and inscribed on the ancient temple of Apollo at Delphi, is "Know thyself."

Second is my relationship to others—my family, my friends, my neighbors, the members of my church, my co-workers, etc. How am I doing with these relationships? Which ones are strong, deep, and healthy? Which ones are problematic and need attention? And what kind of attention do they need? The ancient imperative in this second area, our relationship to others, is to love—as Jesus put it, to "love thy neighbor as thyself."

Third, I think about my relationship to the world. By this, I mean our relationship to the powers and principalities of the world—the dimensions of social justice, advocacy, and service to others. Whether we do anything about it or not, we have a relationship to the hungry and the homeless, to the depressed and the down-and-out. We certainly cannot work on all of these problems at once, but we are all called to serve, and we will never be spiritually whole, I would suggest, without attending to at least some of these problems as a way of having a healthy relationship to the world. The ancient imperative in our relationship to the world, again in the words of Jesus, is to "feed the hungry, clothe the naked, shelter the homeless, care for the sick, welcome the stranger, and visit the imprisoned."

Fourth, I consider my relationship to nature and the environment. This comprises at least two sets of issues. First, are there ways I can, and should, do more to protect the environment? Is my community recycling, cutting back? Are we advocating and voting for environmentally sound legislation and planning? Should we consider vegetarianism? The second aspect of our relationship to nature entails our finding ways to stay connected to the larger, natural interdependent web of existence of which we are a part. This might mean walking in a park or the woods, going hiking, gazing at the stars, and otherwise taking time to appreciate our larger natural environment. The ancient imperative with respect to nature is to respect the environment and to take only what we need.

Finally, the fifth relationship I consider in taking an inventory of one's life is my relationship to the cosmos. This is the big picture of life and death and meaning. What does it mean to be alive and one day have to die? What is the significance of the existence of life on this one, fairly ordinary planet, whirling through space around one of a billion stars amidst billions of galaxies amidst the vastness of space and time and the underlying, irreducible silence? Is there a God and, if so, how do I discern the spiritual significance of God in my life?

In traditional Western spiritual language, the ancient imperative in our relationship to the cosmos is to "Love thy God with all thy heart, and all thy soul, and all thy mind." In Buddhist terminology, the imperative is to "be present." In Taoist language, it is to be in harmony with the Tao. More simply, I think the ancient imperative, here, is to grow in wisdom.

As you systematically survey your life, you are likely to encounter a wealth of material with which to be engaged while at the same time being reminded of at least five worthy imperatives, or purposes, for our lives: to know thyself, to love others, to serve the world, to respect the environment, and to grow in wisdom.

So, indeed, there is plenty to do on a silent retreat, ranging from simply relaxing to contemplating the deeper spiritual significance of the irreducibly elemental nature of silence. Stepping out of the rat race for a weekend of rest and reflection, grieving our losses, pondering important decisions, and taking a comprehensive inventory of one's life are additional options, along with other aspects we may find that need attention. Considering the wealth of worthy material with which to be engaged, it should not be surprising that many silent retreats result in life-transforming resolutions, decisions, affirmations, and tears of both grief and joy.

So, how does one get started on a silent retreat? One way is simply to try it on your own. While you may theoretically be able to do this in your own home or apartment, most people, for a variety of reasons, find it far easier to appreciate the depth and beauty of silence in settings away from home. My first silent retreat, for example, was for a weekend alone at a friend's remote island cottage. Another way I have come to prefer is to find a retreat center that has some experience with silent retreats. For example, I spend a week of silence each summer with about twenty-five others at a retreat center in Door County, Wisconsin. Moreover, there is a subtle, but special, wordless bonding that takes place in sharing extended periods of silence with others. Sharing meals in silence with others is a wonderful experience, too. Other retreat centers with a discipline of silent retreats may be located in books such as *Sanctuaries: The Complete United States, A Guide to Lodgings in Monasteries, Abbeys, and Retreats* by Jack and Marcia Kelly.

Additionally, I go for at least one weekend of silence each year with a group from my local Unitarian Universalist church. And, finally, having had these experiences with silence, I now reserve one morning a week for silence. It may not be much, but it helps me keep my spiritual balance in a wild and crazy world. Even my incredulous brother can appreciate that.

Creating an Altar

Johanna Nichols

When I moved from my home in Vermont to California to go to seminary, two white-veined, black rocks common to Lake Champlain traveled with me. There, I placed them on my windowsill facing the San Francisco Bay. A friend from home came to visit. After she left I discovered she had rearranged the rocks, placing the smaller of the two on the bigger one. They now looked like a seal perched on a rock. Suddenly, my whole perspective of leaving home changed: If my Vermont rocks could adapt to California, so could I. Today these two sacred black rocks sit upon my home altar.

In answer to the question, what must one do to be enlightened, the Buddha said, "Wake up." Life is a spiritual journey that calls upon us to wake up, to become whole. When we are whole, we are awake, aware, and conscious—with senses engaged—in relation to and connected with our environment. In my religion, we are encouraged to "respect the interdependent web of existence of which we are a part."

Whatever the nature of our particular spiritual journey, we practice waking up and becoming aware. We may pray, meditate, chant, sing, drum, garden, read, breathe, do tai chi, yoga, worship, walk, hike, eat mindfully, write, paint, or sculpt. We use these practices for our physical, mental, emotional, and spiritual well-being.

I have always been a collector of sacred objects. For many years, my rocks and feathers and cherished photos sat in various corners of homes I've lived in—on my dresser, on a mantle, a book shelf, and windowsills.

I first discovered the powerful impact that comes from creating a more intentional center of spiritual focus when I participated in a program on women's spirituality called *Cakes for the Queen of Heaven*. Each week, the women in the group brought objects that held special meaning—gemstones, rocks, painted eggs, photos, jewelry, shells, candleholders, and glass and ceramic art—that we used to create an altar in the center of our worship circle.

After the program ended, we continued to meet once a month at my home to celebrate the cycle of the seasons and rites of passage. A round coffee table served as the base of our altar, on which we placed our sacred objects. With our altar as the central focus, we each brought a presence to the circle that was intentional, creative, harmonious, energizing, truthful, joyful, and powerful.

One day I walked with a friend along the Pacific Coast. We were looking for sand dollars to take to her new home in Utah. We spotted a sand shark washed up on the beach. Discovering it was alive, we found a piece of driftwood, slid it under the shark, and carried it between us knee deep into the ocean. We waited for the next wave, and released it. I felt exhilarated as it swam away. Continuing our search for sand dollars, my attention wandered to rocks. I picked up a gray rock with a strange bump on it and turned it over. In my hand lay a perfectly fossilized sand dollar. This 10,000-year-old stone now sits upon my home altar.

Altars hold a central place in the history of many cultures and religions. When an altar is used, it is regarded as a place of contact with the deity, set apart as holy. It might be as simple as a bowl on a stone or a mat. It might be a table made of clay or wood or elaborate bronze or gold.

The Greeks had numerous altars: one in the home for family use, a city altar on which fire continually burned, and a temple altar dedicated to a god. The Hopi constructed sand altars to resemble animals, each symbolizing certain sacred characteristics and relationships with the spirit. In Central America every home had its personal altar. In the evolution of Christianity, increasing ceremony surrounded the eucharistic table after the death of Christ and the altar was moved from the people into the sanctuary.

I spent ten days at a writing seminar at Ghost Ranch in New Mexico where the sky is an ocean of blue and the earth a blanket of red mountain dust. There is no mercy to this geography. To survive in the desert, you must pay attention. Sitting on a rock, I scooped up a handful of earth, mindful that this was once the floor of the ocean, mindful of the ancient feet that had once trod this way. Today, this handful of New Mexico earth sits upon my home altar.

I discovered that between the celebrations of my women's group I wanted to keep the altar intact. In fact, I wanted to create my own altar. I chose a quiet corner in my office as a gathering place for my own sacred objects. An oval coffee table offered a suitable base. A large, round, flat basket with handles, on which to place my objects, would make my altar portable.

I have long been fascinated with the medicine wheel, an ancient symbol used by almost all of the Native people of North and South America to represent the circle of life. The medicine wheel expresses relationships in sets of four: the four directions, races, elements, seasons, stages of life, and aspects of our nature. With the medicine wheel as a guide, I gathered my sacred objects and placed them on the basket to create a center of spiritual focus.

I placed a candle on a piece of quilted fabric in the center of my altar. This candle represents the center (according to the medicine wheel, the transcendent and immanent, Great Spirit and Mother Earth, the Goddess). In the direction of the east (the direction of spring, air, birth, and dawn) I put my collection of feathers in a straw basket and a yellow candle in a glass holder. In the direction of the south (summer, fire, youth, midday) I put the red New Mexico dirt in a clay pot and a red candle. In the direction of the west (autumn, water, adulthood, twilight) I put the fossilized sand dollar, a river rock in water in a small ceramic bowl made by my daughter, and a black candle. In the direction of the north (winter, earth, old age, midnight) I put my black Vermont rocks and a white candle.

Above the altar hang photographs and paintings of special places and handmade symbols of my spiritual journey. Below it, I keep my daily meditation book and my journal for the time I spend there in reflection. All the parts of my center of focus are moveable and changeable. As I continue on my spiritual journey, I add new objects that are sacred to me and give away others. I tend my altar.

In the direction of the south, I have added a photo of a friend far away who needs healing. In the north, I put photos of my wise grandmother Agnes and two of her sisters. Next to them sits a crystal belonging to my friend Sharon. When she died, her husband invited each of her women friends to take something from her personal altar. It was very hard to do, for the altar held a lot of power and integrity that was connected to her. But now her crystal is part of my altar.

My personal home altar is my place to pray, meditate, read, and write in a setting that connects me to the sacred. The world is so temporal that we have to intentionally make it more sacred. I know that I will be awake when I am in the presence of my altar. Its individual objects are sacred to me because of their natural beauty and form, and because of the meanings they hold, the parts of my spiritual journey they evoke. The rock with the fossilized sand dollar was made sacred by the feeling of synchronicity I had when I discovered it. I felt a connection to the shark and the sea and my friend that I experience again whenever I see or hold this rock.

My altar is a touchstone in my life. Though I try to bring awareness to every aspect of my life, from doing the dishes to attending worship, the presence of my personal home altar connects me to the sacredness of life. The sacred objects on my altar call forth the sacred in me that connects with the sacred in nature and with the sacred in worship. It beckons me to pause, to reflect and to regain my sense of balance and wholeness.

My altar can go anywhere with me—on a trip, to a new home, to the hospital or a nursing home. And if sustaining a home altar remains as a personal spiritual practice, when I die, it can be buried with me or dispersed to my family and friends.

Would creating and tending a home altar be a meaningful spiritual practice for you? Ask yourself this: am I a collector? Do I collect sea glass or shells, rocks or feathers? Driftwood? Are there objects that hold meaning for me, that reflect my connection with nature, relationships with other people, a connection to ancient traditions?

Do I like to celebrate? Do I decorate my home for different seasons and holidays? Do I like to keep photos or cards in a place where I can see them? Am I creative? Do I enjoy arranging flowers in a special vase or covering a table or bureau with a colorful cloth?

Do I have a quiet space where I enjoy sitting quietly sometime during the day or evening—perhaps to sip a cup of tea, read a daily meditation, or simply just to sit? Do I sit at a table near a window, on a porch, or in a cozy chair where I can put up my feet?

Whether we do so intentionally or not, each of us creates an environment in our home that nurtures us through our senses—sight, sound, touch, taste, and scent. An altar can nurture you through your senses, add meaning and beauty to your life, remind you that the holy is present wherever we call home.

If you would like more information about designing a center of spiritual focus, the resource section in this book can direct you to other sources. Ultimately, however, your home altar should reflect your personal spiritual story. It doesn't matter whether it consists of a candle, a bell, and a statue of Buddha on a piece of cloth, or a bowl of sea glass and a photo on linen crocheted by your grandmother. It doesn't matter if you pay attention to the directions or just gather your own precious objects and mementos.

What is important is *who you are* in the presence of your personal altar. For there, you have created a place where you are invited to recognize the sacredness of life, where you are invited to "wake up!" and be whole.

Adversity

Barbara Merritt

When searching for a spiritual practice, most of us seek a discipline that will soothe, comfort, relax, and nourish us. The human hunger for inner peace is deep; it is understandable to hope for clarity, harmony, and a calm and pleasant path to reach them. One can't help but wish for a taste of the tranquillity that is being sought.

Yet while many spiritual practices offer all kinds of pleasing, even immediate benefits, there may be no practice as transformative, as effective, and as ultimately beneficial as adversity. Adversity can be defined as that which comes into your life that you would never voluntarily choose. Whatever the particular form of hardship or limitation, adversity is that which, by definition, you do not want. The word adverse comes from the Latin adversus, meaning "hostile." No one could be expected to want or to welcome what is perceived to be harmful. We have an instinctive and healthy desire to avoid that which interrupts and disturbs plans, causes suffering and anguish, or seems to threaten our security, health, and well-being.

Yet every human life encounters adversity. Some people may have less, some more. Some people's hardships are more obvious to the casual observer; others hide their suffering very effectively. But in a creation of good and evil, joy and sadness, birth and death, all souls will find themselves in the midst of some difficult circumstances.

The important question is, What relationship will we have to that adversity? Will we hate it? Will we attempt to escape it, perhaps through destructive addictions to alcohol or drugs? Will we engage in behaviors that are so excessive that they momentarily distract and console us? Will we withdraw into self-pity, depression, or whining complaint? Will we become angry and project our unhappiness onto society, or other external targets? Will we blame our suffering on poor parenting, cultural oppression, historical injustice, or bad genes? Will we take refuge in the belief that, if the world or the economy or our neighborhood could only be transformed, there would be very little hardship in our lives?

There is an alternative. The great schools of meditation and prayer and spiritual discipline agree that it is possible not only to *accept* adversity with forbearance and equanimity, but to use it to more deeply understand what is essential and what is peripheral in life. Adversity can be one of the great teachers of the soul. When the saints of all world religions repeat in one form or another the simple prayer, "Not my will, but Thine, O Lord," they are not denying that all people have desires or that our longing for happiness, ease, and rest is legitimate. Instead, this prayer acknowledges that there is something larger than one's own ego, desire, or intention. Whether or not we believe in God, we must recognize that we ourselves are not God. This prayer is an open admission that our will is not in charge, our desires are not running the world, our preferences are not preeminent. Welcoming "thy will"—however we define " thy"—means that we will accept, trust, and be open to that which is pleasing as well as that which is not pleasing at all.

Rumi, the thirteenth-century Islamic poet and mystic, told a remarkable parable about adversity as a spiritual practice. "Sheikh Kharraqani and His Wretched Wife" appears in *The Essential Rumi,* translated by Coleman Barks. In the story, a young religious seeker heard of one Sheikh who could bestow peace to a conflicted mind with a single glance. He set off on the long journey to the mountains where the Sheikh was believed to live.

The young man arrived at the Sheikh's house and knocked on the door. The teacher's wife stuck her head out of the window and asked, screaming, what he wanted. The young man replied that he intended to see the great, holy teacher, the Sheikh. His wife let loose with a barrage of insults, recriminations, and accusations, calling the Sheikh a parasite and a fraud and the young man a fool. The seeker was taken aback, but undeterred. He told the woman that her angry words could not stop his quest for wisdom. "For you to try to blow out his candle is as futile as for you to try to blow out the sun."

And so the seeker continued his search. He went into town and learned that the teacher was in the forest collecting firewood. The young man hurried to the forest, but now his mind was troubled. Why would an enlightened teacher have such a wretched, miserable wife? Suddenly, the teacher appeared riding on a lion. The teacher had not only the power to quiet and tame the wildest of beasts, but he also read the doubt in the mind of the young man. The Sheikh immediately answered the unspoken question of the seeker. He told the young man that he had not chosen his wife and that he did not desire her company. He was committed to her, but for reasons of his own. "It is not her perfume or bright colored clothes. Enduring her public disdain has made me strong and patient. She is my practice."

In this story, Rumi suggests a whole new way of looking at what is troublesome, difficult, or demanding. "This is my practice." It could be a specific person or your own grumpy, stubborn, self-centered personality. It could be your health, your financial circumstances, your family of origin, or any number of troubles. Adversity may create an enormous amount of grief and sadness. Yet, through it, we may have the opportunity to become stronger and more patient. In the presence of adversity, we are constantly forced to remember our center, our source of ultimate strength, what is most real.

Adversity is rarely chosen, yet it does bring a peculiar kind of blessing. When Jesus spoke about blessings in the

Sermon on the Mount, he did not describe circumstances that we think of as calming or pleasant. The Rabbi said, "Blessed are the poor in spirit." Those who mourn, the meek, those who hunger and thirst after righteousness, those who are persecuted, those who are reviled, and those who are falsely accused are also called blessed. Even the few blessings Jesus mentioned that sound positive are exceptionally difficult to obtain. Being merciful, pure in heart, or a peacemaker requires sacrificing self-centeredness, a diminishment of the ego, a turning away from selfish gratification.

When Jesus said that in order to acquire the "pearl of great price," we must sell all we have, he did not explain exactly how expensive the kingdom of heaven would be to obtain, or how long and painful the journey would be. But he gave plenty of compelling hints. He described the spiritual practice of his teachings as being akin to walking on a razor's edge. He said there would be no safe place to lay your head. He claimed you must become the servant of the "least of them." Jesus was not afraid of adversity. He taught that it was an integral part of God's grace. Jesus was not deterred by the limitations and fears and duplicity of his disciples. Even on the cross, at his own death, he forgave enemies and showed compassion toward the thief dying next to him. He always remembered what was essential. He kept in relationship with his truth.

If all of this discipline and hardship and sacrifice sounds too demanding, too uncomfortable, too difficult, you might wish to turn away from Jesus' teachings and search for easier spiritual nourishment in other world religions. You would be disappointed. This acceptance, even welcoming, of adversity is a common theme in all of the major world religions. The Buddha said, "To my best disciples I give disease, poverty, and dishonor." Apparently the Buddha understood that these hardships are some of the most auspicious circumstances in which to move forward on the path of enlightenment.

The Islamic tradition is especially eloquent about the essential nature of conflict and adversity on a spiritual path.

Rumi, who has been called the Shakespeare of Spirituality, wrote in his epic poem, *The Mathnawi:* "Do not now complain of affliction . . . for it is a smooth paced horse carrying you towards truth." Rumi claims that adversity teaches us lessons that prepare us for a far greater joy. "The thought of sorrow sweeps your house clear of all else, in order that new joy from the source of good may enter in. It scatters the yellow leaves from the bough of the heart, in order that incessant green leaves may grow. It uproots the old joy, in order that new delight may march in from the beyond. Whatsoever sorrow may cause to be shed from the heart, or may take away from it, assuredly, it will bring better in exchange."

What makes adversity a discipline rather than a distraction, a disruption, or the enemy? A discipline, a practice, is a commitment. It is a way of staying in relationship, despite changes in mood, weather, and schedule. When you accept adversity as one of your spiritual disciplines, you recognize it as an integral part of your spiritual practice. You acknowledge that the reality, the truth, and the peace that you seek grow by way of a long and mysterious process. When you directly face the reality that some of what you encounter along the way will be difficult, you stay in relationship with the totality of life.

Some of what you learn will be humbling and distressing. Regardless, you make a commitment to keep your heart open. Some of the circumstances in which you find yourself will make you frustrated and unhappy. It is precisely then that your discipline will allow you to go forward. Adversity will no longer be a stumbling block, but part of the training, part of the transformative process. Life presents us with challenges that are meant to be faced and overcome. Our disciplines reflect our commitments, our willingness to work toward long-term goals. Welcoming adversity as a normal part of one's spiritual life is one way of expressing faith and trust in the possibility that despite the confinement and limitations of the moment, there is greater joy and abundance to come.

While we may have initially hoped that our spiritual practice would provide us safe refuge and solace and an escape from the challenges of the world, the seeker soon discovers that the journey toward truth and reality is the greatest challenge in existence. All of life becomes a teaching. Eventually we will learn to trust all of our circumstances as opportunities for spiritual deepening. Eventually we will learn to be grateful, not only in the best of times but also in the worst of times. We will not wish away our pain, our struggle, our brokenness; we will actually welcome them as occasions of grace.

In the book *The Subject Tonight Is Love*, Hafiz, a fourteenth-century Persian mystic, imagines in his poem "Absolutely Clear" how we might even want adversity to stay with us longer, until we have learned all that we can from our unchosen circumstances. As translated by Daniel Ladinsky, the poem reads:

Don't surrender your loneliness
so quickly.
Let it cut more deep.
Let it ferment and season you
As few human
Or even divine ingredients can.
Something missing in my heart tonight
Has made my eyes so soft,
My voice
So tender,
My need of God
Absolutely
Clear.

Perhaps the most important spiritual lesson we can learn from adversity is our need for something greater than ourselves. Adversity has the power to take away our arrogance, our illusions of control, our delusions of self-sufficiency. Adversity can force us to ask for help. It can bring us into community. It can open our eyes to the grace and the love that have always been present. When life goes too smoothly, we often do not realize how dependent we are. Adversity has the capacity to take us back to the sources of our strength, our truth, and our wholeness.

Many spiritual disciplines require a great deal of intentionality; one must search for, and then cultivate and protect these practices. Adversity, on the other hand, will come to us without any effort or exertion. When difficult circumstances present themselves, we can choose to pay attention. We can keep our hearts and minds and souls open to the gifts of the spirit, which are hidden in the midst of an imperfect world.

The Sacred Moment

Edwin C. Lynn

Creating sacred moments is my spiritual practice. Combining meditation and mindfulness, the sacred moment expresses my religious conviction that life is precious. We are on earth for a finite time. Every day is blessed, and I want to live that day fully. Philosophers and poets encourage us to live in the now, to dwell in the eternal present. I find it difficult to stay that focused. But the sacred moment provides a stopping place, a listening post, where the preciousness of immediate experience and living-in-the-now unite.

When I first became fascinated by sacred moments, I referred to them affectionately as "S moments." Such a moment occurs, for example, each morning, when I stop at a small pond on my way to the office. In order to better remember each phase of the experience, I use a descriptive word that begins with S: sight, followed by sky, stance, smell, sense, and sound.

SIGHT: I look out at the surrounding trees and distant shore. I try to notice new discoveries and to be aware of subtle daily changes in the blossoms, leaves, shadows, and colors. The water changes moment by moment, depending upon the wind and sun. Water is especially sensitive to light, and the breeze creates a ballet of changing reflections.

Human eyes and brains need little time to take in a natural setting. A quick look is enough for most people, and then they move on. Because I have a background in architecture, I have always been conscious of my visual surroundings. But through time I have become aware of the need not only to see but also to engage all of my senses. Whether a building, a natural scene, or any other setting, I want to both see and feel.

I remember my first visit to Chartres Cathedral outside Paris, which was the fulfillment of years of anticipation. We arrived at the cathedral at four in the afternoon; the church closed at five. For the others in the group, this was no problem. They went inside, looked, walked around, and were in the gift shop well before five o'clock.

I couldn't get enough of the building in that short time. I wanted to meditate on the mandala-like rose windows, luxuriate in the colors of the stained glass, marvel at the magnificence of the space, feel the roughness of the stone floors, and touch the soaring stone columns.

With only an hour, I rushed ahead of the sexton as he began closing each of the doors of the vast sanctuary. I knew then that I wanted more than seeing—I wanted a sense of being. I wanted to experience the cathedral more fully. Seeing is our basic instinct, but for a deeper sense of being, I needed a more complete involvement of my senses. I wanted to create a sacred moment.

SKY: Often, we see only what is at eye level, without being aware of the sky. Friends of mine from the Midwest are very mindful of the sky's presence. On the east coast, obscured by urban buildings and rural trees, the sky is not so prominent. Whether it is cloudy or bright, I find that when I am aware of the sky, I am more aware of the day. The sky becomes my symbolic umbrella, a wider context for the day's tasks. I am fascinated that the loss of awareness of the sky is so widespread that an organization called For Spacious Skies was formed and is dedicated to helping adults and children be aware of the beauty and science of the skies. For me, the sky can be a significant reminder of our physical and spiritual presence in the world.

STANCE: As I look out at my surroundings and the sky, I become aware of my stance on the ground, my rootedness and connectedness with the earth. I feel this relationship through my legs and feet. Whether standing, sitting, or walking, I notice the ways that I am centered and grounded. At some instinctive level my recognition of stance connects me to the earth.

SMELL: Smell is the most fundamental of our senses. The nose is the sense organ most directly connected to the brain. As a result, smell can provide deep memories. My own experience tells me this is so. When I returned to New England after a ten-year absence, it was not the landscape or the sky that I remembered most vividly, but the distinctive smell of the dampened leaves nestled in the woods. A delicate sniff can catch the subtle aromas of a pond's misty moisture of natural flowers or of local vegetation.

SENSE: I use the term "sense" to describe the sensation of touch, another part of my sacred moment. I want to feel the temperature, the breeze, or if eating, the taste. Like most people, I used to pay little attention to the wind unless it was very brisk. As I have become more attuned to my senses, I find that most of the time there is a slight breeze, and when I'm particularly aware, I feel it on different parts of my face. Warmth and cold expand my sense of the moment. The feeling of warmth from the sun or the damp chill of penetrating cold is a part of the moment.

SOUND: Sound is the crucial focus of my sacred moment, because listening is both its theme and its essence. As in meditation, by eliminating our mental chatter, we free the mind. Each of us has visited a lake or a mountain and, rather than pay attention to our surroundings, let our minds and thoughts wander. The sacred moment intensifies and lengthens our time of seeing into a time of being.

To reach a sacred moment, I find I need to look relatively straight ahead and not be distracted by any moving sights. I listen to the wind, the leaves, the water, and the birds. With these outer sounds, the chatter of my inner thoughts is kept from intruding upon the moment. If I am not listening, I know I am not in the experience, but still trapped in my head, thinking of the past or the future. Standing at the pond, I see the landscape and the sky, feel the ground and the breeze, and smell the water. Mostly I listen. With purposeful breathing, I can continue the experience.

My day includes other times for sacred moments. In the morning while showering, I don't just get clean, but use the time to create a sacred moment. The sights are obviously limited, and I cannot see the sky, but stance, sense, and smell are particularly acute. Listening to the water as it splashes on my body throughout the shower is the key. When I can stay focused, the shower is not only a more enjoyable experience, but it connects me to the larger waters of the pond, the ocean, and the skies.

I usually eat breakfast using the same sense of focus. I avoid watching early-morning television or reading the newspaper; I have time for those connections later. In the morning, I want to let my heightened awareness engage the glory of the day. I leave for the office a few minutes early in order to stop at the pond. The difficult part is allowing the extra time. It is very easy to rationalize that I don't have the time. But I do stop, and I'm always glad I have.

At midday, I used to go to nearby restaurants to get out of the office. I would usually eat too much of the wrong foods. In the past year, I have been bringing a lunch of healthier selections and often eat in a wooded area near the church to create a sacred moment. At the end of the day, I take the time to go for a walk. This is not just a walk for exercise, with the usual daydreaming; I apply the principles of the sacred moment to create a walking meditation. I find I'm able to sustain a more continuous sacred experience while I'm walking. The sights and sounds are richer, though the distractions are more plentiful. I am especially aware of the sky and of the variation in smells from place to place—even of the wind changing direction along the way. Once again, listening is key to staying in the moment. I listen to my footsteps, the sounds varying according to the season and the surface (dry pavement, wet soil, or crunchy snow).

Sacred moments need not be limited by location, and some—such as being mindful during a morning shower—require only a shift of awareness. Other activities, such as walking meditation, may call for extra time, a greater limitation for most people. I will always remember a meditation teacher asking his students, "If you plan to meditate, what will you give up?" Some people give up sleep, or productivity, or pastimes. If we simply keep adding new activities, we will become overloaded, a state that is exactly the opposite of the quiet of the sacred moment.

I have been creating sacred moments every day for a little more than a year, and I find the preciousness of the day is enhanced in direct proportion to the number of sacred moments I experience. In addition to the intentional moments, I find with my new awareness that I'll be walking in an unlikely location and suddenly realize that I'm aware of the sky and listening to the moment. Through sacred moments, we can quiet our mind's inner chatter, and transform our experience of merely seeing into one of being.

Living by Heart

Laurel Hallman

It was my friend and mentor Harry Scholefield—compassionate pastor, teacher of ministers, activist for peace and social justice—who taught me what I know about spiritual practice. When I was a busy mother and graduate student twenty years ago, Harry encouraged me to make time for my inner life by saying, "If you don't have a devotional life, you will dry up and blow away." In the years since then, the meditative practice Harry calls *living by heart* has enlarged my vision, connected me to the vitality and purpose of life, and helped me to claim the power that is mine—the power to affect the day, and to live, in Henry David Thoreau's words, in "the infinite expectation of the dawn."

Living by heart begins with waiting—with pausing, sitting, looking, and taking time to let something happen within us. For goal-oriented people who structure their days with lists, it can be very difficult to pause without expectation. Most of us are willing to pause, but only if we are sure that there will be results. It takes practice to wait long enough to let something happen within our meditation and in the living of our lives. But this practice sets the foundation for everything else we do.

I began by getting a pillow and sitting outside each morning. Sometimes it was a time of simple rumination. Increasingly, however, it became a time of waiting, watching, and listening. It was time for an inward glance and recollection of who I was most deeply. Often I would find myself coming to a deep sense of gratitude.

It is good to start with a specific time and place for practice—nothing fancy or exclusive, but a place and time where we can go every day—in the sunrise, in the dawn, if we are morning people. Or some other time in which we can reclaim our deepest selves—a place where we can be alone and apart.

The next step is bringing phrases, songs, or poetry into your meditation. Many of us already collect bits and pieces of wisdom—the quotes posted on our refrigerator doors, pinned to our bulletin boards, and tucked in our wallets. Living by heart is an extension of this practice, creating a habit by intentionally choosing and incorporating wisdom words into our daily lives.

Choose words from poetry, scripture, or other reading that you want to incorporate into yourself and to be a part of your life. Learn the words by heart, and let them live within you. (Notice the word *letting* again.) This process is much different than the rote memorization that we might remember from our school days. By learning poetry by heart, we absorb the words into our very beings and let our deepest selves respond to them. As we live with the words, they become part of the fabric of our daily lives.

At first, Harry kept a small notebook of words and phrases that he wanted to learn by heart. He began to take his notebook with him on his morning walks. He said he knew his neighbors must have thought him strange, standing under streetlights before dawn, reading lines in his notebook, but that was how he reminded himself of the phrases and poems he was learning. His book of by-heart poems was not simply a collection of his favorites; the poems it contained were becoming part of him and part of the way he met life itself.

When events and circumstances change, our wisdom words will often take on new meaning and depth. Twelve years ago I was making a serious decision about seeking a new ministry position. I enjoyed my work, but it seemed to be time to move. Harry gave me the poem "My Eyes Already Touch the Sunny Hill" by Rainer Maria Rilke. I sat with the poem in the morning for about two years, letting it sink into my being. It is a poem about the light ahead on a hill that bids us forward and changes us, even if we do not get where we intend to go. It was just what I needed because two years later I found myself in a very different place than I had expected. If I had not lived with the poem, over time, I am not sure I would have been as able to see new possibilities and act with freedom as I made my choices.

Living by heart, then, is forming the habit of living with wisdom words over time and letting them focus our minds and change our hearts.

THE PRACTICE OF WELCOMING

Taking the time to wait, and bringing wise words into your meditation, can transform the way you greet the world. As Harry walked in the early morning light and as he learned poetry and scripture by heart, he realized that he could begin to choose the way he welcomed the day. So many of us greet the day in a habitually fearful or resentful way. Instead, with the help of the words he had learned by heart, Harry began to welcome the day as a gift, even in the midst of pressures and concerns. He began to see the beginning of each new day as a replica of the act of creation. It gave him a fresh view of his life.

As I began to think about how I welcomed the day, I recognized that I woke up each morning to a radio broadcast filled with trouble, from news of wars to mayhem on the highways. While I want to be informed about world and local events, I began to believe that it was not wise to greet the day that way. Instead, I bought a clock that held cassette tapes and chose music to speak to my spirit each morning in the first moments of being awake.

In time, this practice of intentionally greeting the morning can grow into a practice of welcoming every moment. It becomes a way of living with hope. This is not always easy, because there are events and challenges in our lives that we don't want to welcome. It is difficult to welcome the death of a loved one or a diagnosis of illness in our own lives. Wisdom literature shows us, however, that the practice of naming our fears in a spirit of welcoming seems to have been a source of nourishment for people in many times and places. In the ancient Psalms of the Hebrew Bible, the Psalmists often begin by naming despair, moving by the end of the psalm into hope and praise. They trace a pattern for us which it would be wise to follow: acknowledging our fears with a spirit of welcome and, in time, letting our gratitude emerge out of them.

It may seem that such a radical welcome would leave us unprotected when difficult judgments need to be made. Surprisingly, the opposite is true. If we can live in the spirit of welcome, not clinging to fears or outcomes, we can respond with much more freedom and clarity to what life brings than if we live in habitual anxiety and concern.

KINSHIP

Living by heart begins in the concrete, with observations of our surroundings and words on a page. It continues with the imagination, not as an escape into fantasy, but as an awareness of the reality that we are connected to all that is. Living by heart can enlarge our perspective, sometimes in surprising and creative ways.

This awareness of connection often begins with a sense of kinship with the poets and writers whose words you are learning by heart. As he developed his practice, Harry found that poets such as Rainer Maria Rilke, Walt Whitman, and Emily Dickinson became real presences for him. He related to them as friends and mentors and found at times that their various poems were intersecting and conversing as he meditated. He sometimes says as he sits, "Where are you poets?"

"Sometimes they come," he says. "It is as if they come from my heart, where their wisdom lives."

Often meditation is seen as an isolated, autonomous activity that can protect us from the onslaught of tasks and people. But taking wisdom words into our hearts, paying attention to nature, and listening deeply to the wisdom dialogue within is the practice of kinship, not isolation. It draws us into the world, not away from it.

Harry has a related practice he calls *Family Roster*. He sits quietly and calls to mind a picture taken at a family picnic. He recalls each person in his mind, remembering concrete events and particulars about each family member. Seeing each person in relation to the others, and remembering the present in relation to the past, keeps him steady when worries and problems arise. I have adapted this practice to my work; every day I take my calendar and imagine each person, each event of the day to come. It allays my fears and helps me choose joy in my days, rather than crashing through them as if they were simply to be gotten through.

These practices are a good place to begin to cultivate a sense of kinship with others. It is easy to imagine our family members, colleagues, or clients one by one. This sense of You—of another in relationship to us—can be enlarged as we think of a tree in our backyard, or a poet speaking to us across the centuries. It is fostering kinship with all that is.

As the practice of pausing deepens and the naming of the You makes us attentive to our kinship with nature and persons, we become more aware that we are encompassed by mystery beyond naming. We are nourished by more than what we see and hear and know. The practice of kinship opens us to a larger relationship that can be felt but not named. It can be suggested in poetry, but not defined. It can be responded to, but not contained. It nourishes us, like a meal.

This way of being and practice of observing helps us, as the poet Rilke has said, to "rekindle the commonplace." It creates in us, in the words of the Psalmist, "the wine of astonishment." It can also bolster our work in the world, helping us to be active in the political life of our times, by giving us a center of strength on which to build.

PRACTICING LIVING BY HEART

Begin by setting aside a time each day to sit or walk. If you are sitting, set up a special place that is uncluttered. Move outside if you can. If you are a morning person, sunrise is a wonderful time to begin. If you are not, choose another time and place and don't deviate from it. Pause without expectation. If you are walking, do not rush but walk as if you have nowhere to go.

Recall poems and words of scripture and wisdom you already know by heart. Acknowledge the words as they arise from within you, perhaps even from your childhood. In your mind's eye you can open the door of the room within that contains the guiding words you already know.

Notice what you see as you sit or walk. Pay attention. Practice the inward glance and name what you see and feel.

Keep a small notebook of observations. This is not a detailed record, but a simple recording as thoughts and words and sights beckon to you. You may wish to note these observations in terms of your kinship with all that is.

Choose words of wisdom that you want to learn by heart. Copy them into your notebook. Live with the words until they are part of you. Do not rush to memorize them. While it does take some discipline and focus, beware of becoming goal oriented.

Practice the spirit of welcome during your meditative time, welcoming what comes (or does not).

Living by heart begins with pausing, paying attention, fostering a sense of kinship, and memorizing poetry and scripture. In time, it becomes a way of being in the world. It becomes a way of moving into the world with purpose from a center of strength.

Mindfulness

James Austin

The experience of being mindful is not new to any of us. We may not have used the word *mindfulness* to describe our experience, but each waking moment requires some degree of this quality of awareness. We could not function in the world without knowing our experience from moment to moment.

Mindfulness, in this sense, is allowing our experience to be accepted into consciousness, letting us know what we are doing, providing the feedback to permit taking an action, performing a skill, or learning something new. Of course we always know on some level what we are experiencing, where we are, and what we are doing at any given time. It is also true that the degree to which we are really present in our experience varies a great deal throughout the day. There are many moments when the mind seems to be somewhere else completely!

During some moments we are naturally very mindful. Imagine carrying a full cup of hot tea from one room to another. You would pay attention to the cup, being aware of whether or not the tea was about to spill. You might slow down your walking speed or use two hands if you saw that the tea was beginning to spill.

The feedback of knowing what you are doing and the effect on the tea in the cup can all happen because you are present and focused in that moment. If you are thinking about something else while you are carrying the cup (perhaps you are thinking about what you are going to bring from the kitchen on your next trip), then the likelihood of spilling the tea goes up!

There are also some moments when we are usually not very mindful. These moments are likely to occur when we think that what we are doing is not very interesting, or seems automatic because we have done this a thousand times before. So we let the mind drift off while we wash the dishes. "I could have done that in my sleep," we say, and sometimes we did.

You can probably remember a time when you were not very mindful at all. The time you backed the car into a telephone pole while thinking about how late you were going to arrive at an important meeting, or the time you were talking to someone and became distracted by some thought or daydream. Suddenly you realized the person just asked a question that you didn't hear, because you were completely spaced out, miles away from the present moment.

Mindfulness in this sense is a kind of remembering, remembering to be here, to be present, to pay attention to this moment of life. When we bring awareness to this moment we know what we are doing and we know we are alive. It's not so much that our fantasies, daydreams, and desires are not a natural part of life, rather it's that we are so unaware of how much time we spend preoccupied with these thoughts.

Our mind has a mind of its own and easily wanders off into some fantasy of the future or some evaluation, judgment, or remembrance of the past. All this time, we sacrifice what is right in front of us: this present moment. If we do this repeatedly, our minds become a very busy place to live, running back and forth from past to future, while our experience of the present moment becomes shallow and unfulfilling.

As we look more closely at what is going on in our minds we find that we are often trying to do several things at once, usually thinking ahead to the next thing on the agenda. So the first aspect of mindfulness practice in daily life is just to find ways to remind ourselves to show up in the present moment, and to be aware of when we are daydreaming or worrying.

Another aspect of mindfulness has to do with the quality of attention and awareness that we bring to each moment. Even when we think we are being present, we are often so attached to thinking itself that we mistake the thoughts we have about our experience for the experiences themselves. We live our lives very much in words and ideas. Our words and ideas are essential tools, and learning to think and conceptualize clearly is important. One problem with our thinking though, for most of us, is that thinking takes on a life of its own. We are often compulsive thinkers, never giving ourselves a rest from a constant inner conversation. Our stream of consciousness is quite often a stream of thoughts, one following right after another, connected in all sorts of funny, unusual, and unpredictable ways. Other aggregates of consciousness, emotions, sensations, and nonverbal reactions are all given a second class status.

We live in a world of words. In addition to our internal chatter, we receive a constant stimulation of language in the form of the books, advertising, music, news, and conversation. Some jobs require many conversations and verbal interactions to carry on our business during the day. In this context it becomes very easy to unconsciously acquire a belief that thought is consciousness itself—that our experience of the world begins when we think about or label what is happening to us.

When we take on too strong an identification with the thinking mind at the expense of all of our experience, we lose something. What we lose is a sense of direct experience of the richness of life. For example, taking a walk in a garden we see a flower and immediately the label we use follows the seeing in the form of a thought, "rose," followed by the thought, "it seems like they are blooming late this year. It must be the cool spring we had." "I remember last summer when they bloomed my friend was visiting. That was a nice visit. I really should give him a call. I haven't heard from him in a while . . ." Soon we are far away from experiencing the flower in front of us. We may have actually spent only a fraction of a second experiencing the flower in a direct and nonverbal way.

What does this have to do with mindfulness practice? When we take on the intention to be mindful, mindfulness grows as we practice. We are more "present" more of the time. When the quality of mindfulness is stronger, several things happen. We are more likely to see the process of thinking itself, a process we usually miss because we are so identified with the content of our thoughts. In our more mindful moments we see the train of thought and the power that habituated thought has to pull us away rather quickly from the present experience of the flower.

Through the power of being present in each moment, we begin to see that the conceptual processes of labeling, thinking, and evaluating are not the only events that are happening in consciousness in any moment. We begin to value the experience of seeing the flower, of drinking it in through our senses in a nonverbal way. There is a wonderful sense of freedom in this. We may choose to be with the flower, to linger with it for a moment nonverbally to directly experience it, even as our thinking, labeling mind kicks in. We are aware that if we choose to intentionally "be" in a flower garden, our experience will more consciously include both nonverbal experience and thinking at the same time.

When there is too much thinking going on, it is hard to remain open and accepting of our experience. The thinking part of our mind naturally wants to evaluate, wonder, and label. Being in a garden when the mind is restless and busy is not a restful experience. Particularly if it is our own garden! Then much of the experience may be filled with thoughts of the weeding we haven't done, thoughts of planning what we should plant, or thoughts of evaluating how things are growing among others. On the other hand, being in a garden when we are mindful and the thinking mind is quieter, we can directly take in the wonder and beauty of plants or flowers. It is an experience that is likely to leave us feeling more alive and at ease.

Being mindful is not only about becoming more receptive to the outer world. Our inner landscape is more lush when we are more aware. Our reactions to our garden come to us in nonverbal ways, as moods and passing emotions of joy, peace, or perhaps sadness. The emotional content of our experience is always with us, but these nonverbal components of experience are often pushed away to the perimeter of consciousness by our preoccupation with the thinking mind. At those times when the quality of mindfulness is strong, we tend to have a more spacious mind, one which is less dismissive of nonverbal experience.

We have all experienced some time when mindfulness was quite naturally present to a great degree. Perhaps you have experienced this when listening to music or taking in a work of art. It was a time when you wanted very much to allow your present experience to enter fully into consciousness. A time when you were quite content and very much wanted to be in the present moment. Perhaps you were in nature, or with a close friend. The fact is that experiences which we find very fulfilling and rich are often characterized by a high degree of mindfulness. We are interested, we are present, and we are open in these moments.

Sometimes we are very present with an experience that is not necessarily as pleasant as being in a garden. In fact it may be quite unpleasant: a time of intense grief, for example. Intense emotions demand our attention, and we feel very compelled to pay attention to them. When we try to avoid being with an emotion, by distracting ourselves or blotting out the experience with alcohol, we only lengthen the time it takes to work through the difficult emotion.

We can feel very absorbed into a strong emotion such as fear or anger, but we are not necessarily mindful. Mindfulness is characterized by a spacious knowing of what is happening. Anger and fear have the power to take us over, to consume us, so that we find ourselves sometimes doing or saying things we regret later. "I was so angry I didn't know what I was doing," we say. Being more mindful in this situation means that we are more able to know what we are doing. We are able to step back a bit and really know that we are angry. This knowing creates a bit of space that can protect us from acting unwisely. This is not the same as suppressing the anger. In fact, when we are consumed by anger and act out, we often feel like we want to get rid of the anger or the energy behind it. We want to vent it, because it is too difficult to be with. In short, we don't want to *be* with the anger. When we are able to be with it, to receive the experience, to hold it with our awareness even though it is unpleasant, it has less power over us and we are less likely to act out unwisely.

So there are two important aspects to mindfulness. One is knowing what we are doing in the moment and the other is being open to our experience, in a very direct and accepting way. When we take on mindfulness as a practice our intention is to be open to both pleasant and unpleasant experience. We seek through practice to have more mindful moments and less moments of forgetfulness, understanding that to do so requires from us a willingness to be open to our experience. In fact, as mindfulness in daily life grows we naturally experience everything in a more open way. We also learn very quickly that we have a natural tendency to not want to experience unpleasantness. We soon see more clearly what we already know intuitively, that the human animal like other animals recoils from painful or undesirable experiences and is attracted to pleasant or gratifying experiences.

This tendency is so inherent in our nature that we are often not aware of how much energy and effort we put into trying to control our environment so as to collect as many pleasurable experiences as possible and avoid as many unpleasant ones. A higher degree of awareness in our life helps us to see this process, which so often operates in a very mechanical way, more clearly.

Most of us can get by in this way, seeking the pleasant and pushing away the unpleasant, until we reach a time when life won't let us escape from unpleasantness or discomfort. We are all confronted with the changes of growing older, the losses of loved ones, and our fears of approaching illness and death. What happens when we reach a point where we can't get away? We want to resist the changes that come with aging or chronic illness, for example, but the changes come anyway. Our practice can help us to see that though we may not be able to control what is happening, we can learn to work with our resistances.

Mindfulness practice is used in stress reduction and chronic pain clinics around the world because it has been shown that people can often lessen their suffering dramatically by becoming aware of and letting go of their resistance to the unpleasant sensations in their bodies. The automatic response to discomfort in the body is for muscles to tense up, to want to push away the painful sensations. But tension and resistance only create more suffering. If we then add to that a mental script that supports our personal sense of suffering (thoughts of self-pity, for example), we have moved even farther away from easing our situation, by adding mental tension.

By becoming aware of these automatic responses, people can learn to relax and let go of some physical and emotional resistance to their situation. Patients report that they are surprised at how much of their suffering was caused by their physical and mental resistance. When all the extras that are added on to a painful situation are stripped away, so that only the actual physical sensations are left, there can be less suffering.

While a pleasant experience may be easier to be with, and an intense unpleasant emotion or sensation may demand our attention, we have many ways of avoiding less intense unpleasantness. Boredom, for example, might be experienced as intense, but more often than not, it is more subtle. Still, when we are bored we usually run for the nearest distraction, because we see no value in that experience.

Yet, a moment of boredom is one moment of our life, and often when we are patient enough to be even with our experience of boredom, we find it often transforms. We may find that the boredom was acting as a cover for some other more subtle unpleasant emotion that we did not want to experience. There may be something new to learn about ourselves if we choose not to immediately reach for a distraction, not to immediately run from the unpleasantness of boredom. Hiding underneath boredom may be some unease about being alone, or it may be that we have a lot of restless energy in the mind. If we react to boredom mechanically in such a situation, by turning on the television or picking up some reading or eating a snack, we miss the opportunity to see a deeper level of what is true for us in that moment.

We often find that if we form the intention to be more mindful in our lives, to be more present more of the time, then other beneficial qualities of mind also get stronger. For example, when we begin to see that our unpleasant experiences can teach us, and that there can be some value in expending less energy to resist what is in reality an inevitable part of life, we can afford to be more patient with our life and to find more contentment with it.

As we become more patient with our experience, there is less tendency for the mind to race around restlessly. We broaden ourselves to let more of our experience in, to value both verbal and nonverbal experience. We allow ourselves to be more rather than to feel as society often tells us that we are only valuable according to what we do. By being in a deeper and richer way, we connect directly with that inherent self-worth that is our birthright.

GETTING STARTED

So what does a mindfulness practice look like in day-to-day life? It is very much an individual thing. Setting aside some time each day to be intentionally quiet and present is a common thread. For myself, I know that if I miss my morning meditation, the quality of my day is often noticeably different. The other practice that many people find helpful is to find various ways throughout the day to pause and re-center, checking in to see what's happening in the present moment. Do I feel tense? Do I feel relaxed? Am I worrying about something that may or may not happen? Am I holding on to a regret about something that has already passed?

Pausing to take a deep conscious breath or two can be helpful. Taking a break for a cup of tea, intentionally focusing the attention on just the simple act of drinking rather than allowing the mind to wander around, can have the effect of re-centering and refreshing us, while strengthening mindfulness. Thich Nhat Hanh, the great Vietnamese Zen master, has suggested a phone meditation where we treat the ring of the telephone like a meditation bell! When the phone rings we remind ourselves to take a deep breath, to be fully present with the caller. Walking can be an opportunity to practice being present, just feeling the sensations of walking as the body moves, choosing not to think ahead to the next thing we will be doing. Just breathing and walking have a wonderful power to refresh us. My walk from the train to the office helps me start the work day refreshed—when I remember to be mindful.

Mindful walking and sitting meditation practices are common to a number of Buddhist traditions. Buddhism values mindfulness practice because, through increased awareness of each experience, we also gain deeper insight into the nature of things—in particular, how all phenomena are impermanent and interconnected. Buddhist teaching holds that a deep insight into these truths will lead to greater happiness, but it must be an insight that comes from direct experience, not from intellectually understanding that everything changes. It is not necessary to become a Buddhist to draw on this rich source of spiritual practice that supports the development of mindfulness. There is something wonderful about the knowledge that for at least 2,500 years, people have been practicing in this simple way.

One technique drawn from Zen and Theravada Buddhist practices involves using breathing as an object of meditation. Here are some introductory meditation instructions for a sitting mediation using the breath:

You may sit in a chair, on a bench, or on the floor. If you are sitting on a chair, choose one where you can sit up straight in a comfortable position. A straight-backed chair is good. Avoid a soft, cushy chair where it will be hard to keep a good posture. You may open your eyes or close them. If you sit cross-legged on the floor, you may want to sit on a cushion for support and to help your posture. Sitting quietly with a straight back, find a location in the body where the sensations of breathing are prominent. For many people this is at the nostrils, for others this will be the sensations of breathing that cause the abdomen to rise and fall with each in and out breath. For the period of time of the meditation, choose to allow the mind to be with the breathing. Allow it to be with the sensations of breathing in, and then the sensations of breathing out, whatever they might be. If the mind wanders—and it will—do not be disturbed by this. It does not mean that you are a bad meditator.

Beginning meditators are often quite surprised at how busy the mind can be when left on its own. Just gently remind yourself to return from wherever the mind has been—in the past which has already gone by or the future which has not yet come—and return the attention to the experience of the breath in the present moment. After some minutes the mind will calm down on its own and be more willing to be fully present, even with something as simple as just sitting and breathing. Sometimes, the mind is very restless and filled with a torrent of thoughts. One way of working with this is to count the breaths, counting each in breath from one to ten and then starting over. Another way of working with this situation is to use a syllable to give the mind a little more work to do, so that it will be less distracted. Say silently to yourself, "In" on the in breath and "Out" on the out breath, or choose something more meaningful if you like, such as "peace - ful." When the mind calms down, you can drop the syllables.

Try to develop a regular practice, even if only for a short time each day. Ten or twenty minutes may be enough to start. Later you can always increase the length of time that you sit. If you can find one or more friends who are interested, it can be very supportive to practice together. A local meditation center can also help to support your practice.

When we see the richness that practicing mindfulness can impart to our lives, we understand that whatever spiritual practices we choose to take up, being more mindful can help us to work with those practices more deeply, because we are simply more present, more directly in contact with whatever is going on in the present moment. In fact, when we look closely at our practices, we often find that we are drawn to them because they help us to reconnect to the present, to this very moment of life.

Sitting Zen

James Ishmael Ford

It was the end of our first Wisconsin winter, my first spring serving a suburban parish near Milwaukee. I glanced across the now greening grass at my old concrete Ho-tei, a statue given to my wife and me by a former congregation. Jan and I had lived with him for a number of years, and over the years had become very fond of him. But the rigors of winter had been too much for him. An enormous crack ran from the ground right up to his neck.

It was a small disappointment, certainly not one of the terrible things that mark all our lives. Still, I felt the loss of something I'd come to be familiar with and quite fond of and with which I associate many memories. Then, I found myself reminded of something Achaan Chah Subato, the great Theravadan meditation master, once said about a broken glass. It is one of those sayings that sometimes catch us, and perhaps can mark our consciousness forever more. In fact, I have it in calligraphy and framed and hanging on a wall in my office:

"One day some people came to the master and asked, 'How can you be happy in a world of such impermanence, where you cannot protect your loved ones from harm, illness, and death?' The master held up a glass and said, 'Someone gave me this glass, and I really like this glass. It holds my water admirably and it glistens in the sunlight. I touch it and it rings! One day the wind may blow it off the shelf, or my elbow may knock it from the table. I know this glass is already broken, so I enjoy it incredibly.'"

I've been a student of Zen for thirty years now. Zen meditation is my core spiritual practice. I do it because of that broken glass, because of that crack running through my Hotei. My life, like so many of our lives, has been marked by death and suffering. I look around and I see our existence rising and falling, and I feel pushed into a serious and sustained exploration of the essential nature of it all.

For me this has come down to doing two things. The first is *shikantaza,* or "just sitting." It is the primary meditation practice of Zen, and as the name says, it involves just sitting. This is not a passive practice. Rather, in sitting, one tries hard simply to be aware. And in so doing a dynamic process rises where the various things of our lives, out in the environment and from deep within our bodies, is each revealed.

As a complement to this, I am also a koan practitioner, which is another aspect of Zen training. Koan comes from the Chinese *Kung-an,* or "public case," as in a public document. Koans are stories and brief statements that become objects of meditation and present the opportunity for brief and deeply intimate conversations with a spiritual director. To engage a koan is to allow the possibility of awakening to the real nature of things.

So, each in their own way, shikantaza and koan study help me to understand the actual nature of this "already broken" that marks all things. It is a lesson that is eternal and, in some ways, must constantly be relearned. There is part of us that recoils at transience and wishes against all things to be permanent.

Zen meditation is a medicine against this illness of clinging to the passing as if it were permanent. Now, while I meditate regularly and go on intensive retreats frequently, the proof of this practice comes out in daily life. Zen really is about living our lives each moment by that moment, each day by that day.

The spring I found my broken Ho-tei had been a rough one. Members of my family had been quite ill. One friend was diagnosed with cancer. Others were suffering various setbacks in their lives. And too many people had died. The deaths were the hardest for me.

Always it is complicated. In a very few cases the death had been what can be called good. There was enough time to draw affairs to a close and to communicate messages to those who needed them. And when the time came loved ones were there. Other times this wasn't the case. There were totally unexpected losses—accidents or blindingly quick illnesses. Sometimes these deaths were marked with feelings of bitterness and regret that will never be addressed with any satisfaction.

And so, in that bright spring afternoon, that season of renewal, of rebirth, of new hope, I found myself thinking about loss, and how precious and precarious all things are. This is true of glasses and concrete statues, of pets, of lovers and spouses, of parents and children, of siblings and friends. It can be very hard to just enjoy it incredibly.

This is where I find my old friend my spiritual practice so very helpful. Even though this practice is physically demanding—traditionally one sits in a lotus or half-lotus position on a pillow on the ground, for half-hour to forty-five-minute periods—I've found it worth experiencing the difficulties. It's important to emphasize the difficulties. These difficulties are both physical and mental, and they are the hard way of spiritual discipline.

To attempt to sit silently and be aware is to become aware. And what we become aware of is a jumble mush of dancing monkeys. Our minds are filled with thoughts and emotions racing and raging. When we actually sit and notice, we discover much about ourselves, and a fair amount of it isn't particularly pleasant.

But as the mind quiets a bit, other things are also revealed. We begin, perhaps, to notice the many springs of our lives. Not only are there difficulties and endings, but there are also beginnings. This slowing down and noticing is an opportunity. And this opportunity is a chance to notice the passingness of things, the precious fragility of everything.

We can see it in a single blade of grass, a much loved coffee mug, a fading photograph, a quick kiss.

When we attend, really attend, we may find all moments speak of the wonder and transitoriness of life and death within the interdependent web. This certainly has been true for me. I've found that, as hard as it can be to face, there are beauty and wonder in this existence. The simple truth is that this very moment is the only place we will find joy and love and meaning.

Whenever I'm reminded of this I realize how grateful I am for my practice and my spiritual guides; and I realize it is time to hug a child, to pack a lunch and take a walk, or to have that conversation with an old friend I've been putting off. I just need to be reminded, and my Zen practices are the truest of the many reminders I've ever had.

Perhaps we all need such reminding. I suspect this is so. Certainly, as we notice the breath, we find a new season, a new beginning. With each breath, with each moment noticed, we find hope is within us. And, this hope may reign so long as our blood pounds through our bodies.

What I've come to believe, with my bones and marrow, is that it is all revealed here and now. But because of our clinging to what is passing as if it were permanent, we miss what is actually going on. We need to wake from the drowsiness of clinging. We need to wake up. Zen is all about waking up.

The great American Zen master Robert Aitken recently retired from active teaching. During the celebration of his years of service to Zen and to our Western communities, he was asked "What is Zen?" Without blinking an eye, he said, "Zen is minding your own business, and flossing every day."

My spiritual practice of Zen meditation and frequent Zen retreats is about noticing the luminous quality of the ordinary. I sit still and notice. I engage in koan study and notice. And what I notice is how everything is already broken and that it is there to be enjoyed incredibly. This noticing and enjoying includes glasses, and concrete Ho-teis. And it also includes you and me.

The great play of the cosmos, our rising and falling, is the precious web of existence. When we take up a practice like Zen, we can come to know this as liberating, as freeing, as our true heritage. We so easily get caught up in the mix of things. Do this, do that. We need to pause and to remember the glass really is already broken.

This pause is important, because it awakens us. For me that pause is found most frequently, most truly, because of my Zen training, my Zen practice. We each of us can, of course, find it in a myriad of ways.

But however we do it, I hope we will completely engage that pause. This pause is an invitation, a call to enjoy it incredibly! Minding our own business closely, and doing what needs to be done, is the way of the already broken. It is the way of Zen. It is the way of the perfectly ordinary. And it is an authentic spirituality for our times.

Monastic Practice

Wayne B. Arnason

4:15 a.m. My watch alarm wakes me up, just before one of the other men in my dorm turns on the overhead lights. There is no time to lie in bed and consider how I feel. We have less than half an hour to prepare for the day, eat breakfast, and be ready to walk up the hill to the cabin where we will be sitting zazen for ten hours. This exercise is called Tangaryo. It is one of the barrier gates through which one must pass to become a student of Zen Mountain Monastery.

4:45 a.m. The four of us who will undertake this all-day sitting meditation meet our monitor and walk up the hill together. It is December, and sunrise is a long way off. The air smells like snow, although none is falling yet. With flashlights in hand, we trudge through the slush across the field to the steep path up the hill.

4:55 a.m. The cabin is still chilly, but there is a roaring fire in the wood stove. Two of the monastery residents have already been here to start the fire. The room is empty except for an altar and sitting pillows (zafus) facing the walls. There is an outhouse around the corner from the cabin. We are told we can use the outhouse and change our sitting positions whenever we want. At noon we will break for lunch. Several of us stretch out or pace in these last minutes before we start. We are nervous. "All right," says the monitor, "let's start sitting."

When I learned that an all-day meditation was required to become a student of this monastery and of its resident teacher, Daido-roshi, it seemed beyond anything I could possibly undertake. Although I have been meditating using various forms for twenty-five years, a consistent Zen Buddhist meditation practice has only been part of my life for the past three. I am easily distracted by the pain in my legs and ankles when I sit for the thirty-five-minute periods that are part of the daily practice and liturgy of the monastery. Sitting for ten hours felt impossible to me.

Sunrise: We have been discouraged from bringing watches into the cabin. The only ways to mark the passage of time are the changes in light, the feelings in your legs and ankles that suggest it's time to change positions, and the activities of the monitor stoking the fire and lighting new incense.

If it's sunrise it must be seven o'clock or so. I have been restless. It is hard to quiet down.

Aside from the usual suggestions about how to meditate, the residents and students of the monastery who are here this weekend gave me few clues about what to expect or do. There was, however, one resident whose face lit up when I told him I was here to sit Tangaryo. He said to me: "Enjoy it! You may never get to sit like this in the same way again! For the first time, you are completely in charge of your body and what it needs to be comfortable. Combine this with all that time stretching out in front of you, and it's a great opportunity." I hear his voice saying these words as I switch positions. I look out the window. It is starting to snow.

As I look back at it now, the apprehensions and preconceptions I felt about sitting Tangaryo mirror the apprehensions and preconceptions I had about taking up Zen practice at all. I speculated: Was something mystical or profound supposed to happen? If it didn't, did that mean I was inadequate to this teaching? Would I have the stamina to undertake the practice? Would I find out something about myself that I didn't want to know?

Noon: "It's twelve o'clock," says the monitor. "Time to go to lunch." I find this totally incredible. I have been trying to avoid measuring time, but my best guess was ten o'clock.

I am two hours off ! I have needed to use the outhouse only once, and I have been sitting comfortably in each of the three positions I am using for much longer than I expected I could. Counting the breath has been easier and quieter than it was before sunrise. I am surprised to find I go to lunch with mixed feelings. I am hungry, but the break feels like an interruption.

Lunch is ordinary and a feast of experience. We don't talk to the other residents, and we try to stay alert and maintain our practice during the meal. The food is beautiful and delicious. The conversation around us is trivial and profound. The flowers and art that decorate the room are the same and different. Now it is time to go back to the cabin.

Afternoon: The light. The wall. The snow falling and melting on the other side of the window. The sound of the fire in the stove. The breath. One. Two, three. Four, five. "This is wonderful." Uh, oh, back to One. Two, three. Four, five. Six, seven. Eight, nine. Ten. The breath. One . . . . Quiet and ordinary. There is nothing more to be said.

"Four o'clock." "Time to stop." "Congratulations." We go to have tea with Roshi.

My spiritual practice is zazen, the meditation discipline that is at the heart of Zen Buddhism. I practice zazen with the support of a monastic community five hundred miles from where I live. Like thousands of other North Americans, I grew up with a church affiliation and involvement but with an eclectic commitment to spiritual practice. My Unitarian Universalist church community has provided me with many opportunities to explore different disciplines. In midlife I have turned to a monastic tradition for guidance and support in how to deepen my spiritual practice.

Meditation is possibly the easiest of spiritual disciplines to do anywhere. Books and tapes about it abound. It is also an obviously solitary discipline. Why, then, do I drive nine hours one way several times a year to silently do something with a group of monks and students that I can do silently at home every day? The answer to this question from within the Buddhist tradition lies in the fact that Buddhism is like a

three-legged stool. It is supported by three "refuges," as they
are called, sheltering realities that sustain one's practice. The
first refuge is the Buddha, both the historical Buddha and
the Buddha nature that all things share. The second refuge
is the dharma, the teachings of the Buddha. Dharma can
also be understood to mean all the aspects of the universe
and our daily lives in which we find the teachings present or
illuminated. The third leg is the sangha, the community of
people who practice together, not only in a particular place
and time, but throughout space and time. All three are important, but what I was missing through much of my twenty-
five years of sporadic meditation practice was a sangha.

The sangha includes both the teacher and the community
of fellow practitioners. Unlike some Buddhist temples or
retreat centers or sitting groups, a monastery features the
presence of a resident teacher with a clear line of succession
to a tradition of earlier teachers. This was an important element to me when I was deciding to seek out a monastic
setting.

Coming to terms with the fact that I needed a teacher
was not easy for me. As I considered what it meant to admit
I needed a teacher, I had to confront many old images and
expectations of who I was. I am a grown-up! (Kids have
teachers, grown-ups don't!) I was raised and continue to be
a member of a liberal church tradition. (We build our own
theologies!) Ultimately, what was hardest was admitting to
myself that I didn't know what I was doing. In spite of all
the sitting, the retreats, and the books, I really didn't have a
clue what it would mean to live and act from within my true
nature, without the intervening screen of conditioned
thoughts and feelings that keeps me judging, analyzing, and
planning. So I decided I needed to find a teacher.

No matter where your spiritual home lies, whether it be
within Jewish, Christian, free church, Buddhist, or philosophical traditions, there are teachers available to you, once
you accept the need to have one. Because Zen is understood
to be a teaching that happens mind to mind, "a transmis-

sion outside the scriptures," Zen teachers are part of a lineage of teachers going back thousands of years. Some of these lineages have come to America. My teacher, John Daido Loori, is an heir of several of these Japanese lineages. He himself is an Italian American, with a personality that is thoroughly American.

Many teachers are affiliated with monasteries, and there are many options for exploring monastic life and its practices. Although my particular experience has been with Zen Buddhism, Christians (particularly those in the Roman Catholic, Episcopalian, and Lutheran traditions) have long been aware of opportunities for study and practice within their monastic communities. Many monasteries within various traditions are open to lay involvement through structured group retreats or as individuals. Even though some of these monasteries house orders of monks that are either exclusively male or female, their retreats are usually open to people of both genders. A local congregation will likely be able to give you information that will help you find a monastic community in your own part of the country that offers retreats or spiritual instruction.

The monastery that Daido-roshi has founded in Mount Tremper, New York, is unusual—but not unique—in that it has a clear commitment to supporting lay practice. Zen Mountain Monastery has all the characteristics of a traditional Japanese Buddhist monastery. There is a resident roshi ("old venerable master") who is the abbot, and there is a community of monks who live there full time and have taken spiritual vows within their tradition.

We might expect monasteries to be places of quiet. Yet, on most weekends, Zen Mountain buzzes with activity as students of the monastery and inquirers from all over the country arrive for workshops and retreats. Most of these visitors will never be monks. They are drawn nevertheless to this monastic training center for its atmosphere, its structure, the quality of instruction and support they find there, and by the fact that the monastery asks something of everyone. If you are simply attending a retreat, and have paid a registration fee, you are nevertheless expected to participate in the life of the monastery, including its work schedule, while you are there.

Some students find their experience of practice on retreats so compelling that they consider entering the monastery as residents. While different monasteries will have their own traditions, policies, and rules that apply to people who want to explore the monastic life, most require a period of postulancy and training. Monastic vows are usually taken in several stages because the community wants each person to be very clear about the commitment they are making.

I have chosen a different path, becoming a formal student of the monastery. As students we commit ourselves to a Zen practice in our lives at home. We are expected to complete the barrier gates, sustain a relationship with a training director, attend two week-long "sesshin" retreats each year, and pursue our practice in each of eight different areas of training. The monastery supports home practice through books and other resources as well as relationships with the teacher and training director.

Becoming a student is a demanding program of spiritual training, and it is not for everyone. As a student, making time for daily practice has been my most common struggle. It involves getting up early each day to allow a clear space of time before any personal, family, or professional obligations can interfere. Each morning when I get up I do my necessary ablutions and then do about half an hour of yoga stretches and exercises to shake off the stiffness of the overnight. Then I go through a routine of chants from the liturgy of the monastery, and a period of sitting, all of which can take from half an hour to an hour of time. Then I am ready for my day. Less regularly, I will also sit at night before I go to bed. Each time I sit, I truly feel as if I am "taking refuge."

My teacher encourages me to make a space for my practice in my home. I am fortunate to have a small room available to be a meditation room. In the meditation room I have built an altar that is a focal point and a home for the symbols that are found on the altar in the zendo at the monastery. I have my sitting cushions in front of the altar and many of the books about Zen that I own I also keep in this room.

When you begin zazen, the practice usually involves counting your breath for twenty to thirty minutes once or twice each day. When I began, I found myself constantly becoming aware of thoughts and then coming back to start the count over again at "one" every time my mind wandered. Some days, there would be fewer thoughts. Occasionally, things would get very quiet and empty.

This practice is a daily lesson in the second noble truth of Buddhism, that the cause of suffering is attachment. What I find over time is that as I am less attached to my thoughts, the quiet and emptiness slowly start to be more available in other activities of my day. I am slowly becoming a calmer, less driven person. I remember to be fully present to the tasks and people who I am with more often than I ever have before. I find the practice makes a difference in my life.

When I am able to go to the monastery, my practice deepens in many ways. The opportunity for formal interviews with Daido-roshi, the interaction with the resident monks, the chance to compare notes with other students, and the power of the sangha itself all contribute to a greater ease with and commitment to sustaining the practice.

If you are interested generally in meditation, books and workshops can provide an introduction. At some point, however, book instruction is not enough if you are serious about wanting to make spiritual practice a routine part of your life. If you find that your experience is leading you in this direction, I urge you to be in contact with a training center or monastery and explore what they have to offer.

Sacred Reading

Susan J. Ritchie

"Take, read!" are the words that Saint Augustine, that famous debauchee, hears at the moment of his conversion, perhaps the most famous in all Christendom. Rushing to the Bible, Augustine allows it to fall open where it may. His eyes are immediately caught by the passage in Romans that urges the sinner to abandon the ways of dissipation and lust in favor of the Lord. The rest, as they say, is history.

I myself have heard the command to "take, read!" in many ways in my lifetime. I have been a shameless consumer of texts of all sorts: of nineteenth-century novels, colonial British travel diaries, French philosophy, rabbinic theology, cereal boxes. Reading has always had an important role in my life—as escape, as education, and sometimes even as edification. But it was not until I became a professional reader that I had to confront the relationship of reading to my spiritual life.

In my mid-twenties, I completed a doctorate in English that credentialed me, I felt, as a professional reader. I could plow my way through an impressive amount of material in a relatively short time. I prided myself on being able to move through texts of all sorts, quickly identifying the valuable nuggets and throwing all else to the side. It took me longer to realize that I was not reading as much as strip mining. It took even longer to recover a way of reading that enhanced rather than impoverished my sense of the wholeness and beauty not only of the text but also of everything within and beyond my own self.

Since that time I have engaged in the spiritual practice known as sacred reading. The process has been empowering. I have not become, I should say from the start, any less of a critical reader. Sacred reading is not anti-intellectual reading. And yet my approach is different than it was in my days of high-yield mining. With sacred reading, the mindfulness given to the text translates not into product but into a reminder of the power and holistic character of the life within and beyond me. And I would not be exaggerating to say that in the process of engaging in this spiritual practice, something hitherto silent has been given voice within me.

Jean Leclercq, in his work on monastic culture of the middle ages, *The Love of Learning and the Desire for God,* quotes a Cistercian brother giving advice to his fellow monks. For me, this good brother says it all: "When he reads, let him seek to read for savor, not science. The Holy Scripture is the well of Jacob from which the waters are drawn which will be poured out later in prayer. Thus there will be no need to go to the oratory to begin to pray, but in reading itself, means will be found for prayer and contemplation."

And indeed, the form of reading that I practice as an everyday spiritual discipline is not all that different from the *lectio divina,* or sacred reading, that since the middle ages has been an important mainstay of the Christian monastic tradition. True, my practice is not without its peculiar and particular modern twists. Yet the stages of the discipline are the same: the selection of the sacred Scripture, the reading of the text out loud, the memorization of the text, and then, finally, the meditation on the text. If you are interested in practicing sacred reading, it is precisely these steps that I would recommend to you.

Selection of an appropriate text is the first step. It would be most obvious to select some authorized scripture from one of the world's great religious traditions as the object of your sacred reading. But be careful, for in the practice of sacred reading, the obvious poses a special sort of danger.

Walker Percy, in his despair over the inefficacy of American education, once wished that one day students might walk into their high school biology classes to find not a dead frog, but a Shakespearean sonnet carefully pinned to their petri dishes. The point is well taken: We are prepared for most of what we read by a context that already includes within it instructions as to how the text is to be received. "One of the best novels of its generation," the book jacket gloats. "The most significant examples of the sixteenth-century sestina," the teacher intones. In both cases, our chances of a fresh relation to the text are impaired. So however you choose your text—whether it be scripture from one of the world's sacred traditions or from the *New York Times* bestseller list—however you select your passage—whether it be by lectionary, inclination, or random chance—the only requirement is that you be prepared to be surprised.

Once you have selected your text, you can begin by reading it out loud, over and over again. This might seem bizarre at first; it runs counter to our modern understanding of reading as an activity that occurs within the silence and isolated safety of our own heads. Indeed, what harried commuter has not used reading as a way of regaining a sense of privacy even on the most crowded of buses, trains, or planes? But as one of the goals of sacred reading is precisely to restore a sense of bodied-ness to the reader, it is important to read the words out loud. This is to return to a medieval practice of reading, where reading was done not with the eyes, but with the lips. Reading aloud allows the sounds to pull you from the safe confines of your head, back into your body, back into a fuller and fully sensual experience of the world and the text.

The mouth is the most important organ for this process, for what, finally, is sacred reading but a form of eating, an ingestion of other-than-earthly food? Jean Leclercq, the aforementioned scholar of monastic traditions, has noted how often reading is referred to in spiritual literature of the middle ages as a form of *ruminatio*, or rumination—a richly expressive word whose primary meaning is to chew the cud. The words must be felt in the mouth; they must be masticated before they are thoroughly and wholly taken in.

"Take, read"—how reminiscent these words are of the central words of the Mass, "Take, eat!" But the text is a different sort of holiness than the host. The host is not for chewing; it is to remain intact. It is an introjection of holiness. The text, in contrast, is there to be taken apart and put back together a thousand times over. In reading, the holy lies not in the object, but in the activity and experience of the reader.

So speak the text out loud. Hear the sensuous combination of sounds: Hear them first not as mere vehicles of meaning, but as sounds. Feel how good it is to say them. Feel the mouth work its way around the vowels, feel the force of the consonants. Enjoy the very materiality of language. And repeat your passage over and over again. See if you cannot learn your text by heart.

Memorizing texts is, unfortunately, one of those things that has begun to take on the air of a stale classroom. How many of us were forced to memorize some ragged bits of verse by a doctrinaire teacher who cared not a whit for what those syllables truly spoke? But to learn a text by heart, to know it, as we say, backwards and forwards—this is an important element of the spiritual discipline of reading.

For it is in learning a text by heart that we truly remember it, that we truly begin the work of taking those well-chewed syllables and integrating them anew with each other and with our own selves. I have a friend, raised in no particular religious tradition, who when in a difficult or distressing situation finds himself mouthing under his breath a confused combination of the Twenty-Third Psalm and the Pledge of Allegiance. The result is both ludicrous and oddly comforting.

Perhaps it is not so strange that we should find such comfort from words repeated and remembered, for in the process words (oh so generous words) allow us to live for a while within their own music and their own rhythm. For a while we are embodied not only within our physical selves but also within time. Reading can extend the present moment and make it habitable. Those moments when we allow the text to animate us are a blissful relief from our usual sort of existence.

For a while I served as a chaplain on a hospital ward of Alzheimer patients, most of them quite advanced in their illness. Little would restore these patients to anything that we fully remembering adults charged with their care recognized as presence—little, that is, but the Lord's Prayer, memorized by those folks as many as ninety years ago. Something sacred indeed was present when a roomful of desperate human beings, each lost in his or her own universe, would nonetheless come together, every last one of them, on "thy kingdom come, thy will be done, . . ." only to have the brief light of presence flicker away at the end of the recitation.

The final step in the practice of sacred reading is the act of meditation on the remembered text. We have lost through a thousand careless usages the original meaning of this profoundly spiritual act, this meditation. Now, we say we meditate whenever we allow ourselves to drift into the realm of the abstract. But originally, in both rabbinic and monastic contexts, it was only possible to meditate on remembered texts. The act of meditation was a grappling with, a working of, the text by one's understanding and will.

Various contemporary practitioners of this time-honored art would recommend you do this reading in different ways. Some ask that after reading your passage you spend time imagining it: that you recreate it, as well as you can, complete with sights, sounds, and smells, within your own mind. Others suggest a slightly more fanciful approach: that you free associate on the text, that you bring to mind the events in your own life that seem similar to the passage, that you imagine the scene from the vantage point of different characters. Or you can try to feel the passage, deliberately using it to evoke and explore particular emotions. In time, you will find your own way of engaging the text.

Annie Dillard, in her incomparable work *Teaching a Stone to Talk,* describes her encounter with Larry, a man who is trying to teach a stone—a palm-sized, grey beach stone—how to pronounce certain words. Larry is very patient with his work and realizes that his task will probably take several lifetimes to see success. And yet he persists.

Dillard does not describe Larry in order to ridicule him. Rather, she simply points out that he is performing perhaps the most basic gesture of human spirituality. He is trying to say hello to something outside of himself. The joy of sacred reading is that it is finally a way of giving voice within to something that was originally without.

Prayer

Erik Walker Wikstrom

Like many people today, I am something of a religious eclectic. I was raised in liberal Presbyterian and Methodist churches (or, more accurately, in their summer camp programs). I read Richard Bach's *Illusions: The Adventures of a Reluctant Messiah,* Herman Hesse's *Siddhartha,* and the works of Carlos Castaneda and Joseph Campbell. I have been drawn deeply to Buddhist teaching and practice and find much of power and beauty in Wicca and other Earth-centered traditions.

The thread that has run through all of my spiritual wandering has been an interest in the mystical, the belief that the Transcendent can be touched, that Ultimate Reality can be directly experienced. I have always been interested in the disciplines that various religious traditions have developed to facilitate (or, perhaps, train for) this experience. Yet I've often been frustrated because these practices, having been developed within a specific religious context, frequently feel particular to that context. To use them felt like inappropriate appropriation, and the fit was never quite right.

Several years ago, I began developing my own prayer practice. I tried to develop a practice free of particular metaphors and images, not tied to a specific religious worldview, and not demanding adherence to any one set of religious symbols and expressions. Said positively, I wanted to develop a framework that could support a variety of religious beliefs, without depending on any in particular.

I decided to focus on the process of prayer, on its form rather than its content, on the "how" of prayer rather than the "why" or "to whom." Having looked at prayer practices in a variety of religious traditions, I found that a few types or forms of prayer kept coming up. Christianity calls them praise, thanksgiving, confession, contemplation, and intercession; these same forms can be found by other names in nearly all of the world's religions. By using these common prayer forms as the foundation of this practice, I believe that Christians, Buddhists, Neo-Pagans, Atheists, and even eclectics can use it to create a prayer experience that makes sense within their own tradition(s) and understanding.

The practice I developed makes use of prayer beads. Beads have been used as a tool for spiritual discipline in many religious traditions—the rosary of Catholicism and the 108-bead Malas of Buddhism are two well-known examples. Beads bring a tactile involvement to prayer and provide focus and direction. This practice makes use of twenty-eight beads—a large centering bead and four medium-sized beads each separated by a string of four or five small beads—strung so as to make a circle.

The central metaphor of this practice is "prayer as journey." Whatever else it might be—a conversation with the Divine, an internal dialog, a practice of calming and centering—I think of prayer as a movement into and through the Mystery. The beads are strung in a circle to remind us that this is not a linear journey nor a one-time-only event; we end where we began, and then we begin again. This prayer bead practice is designed to help weave together the types or stages of prayer experience, facilitating this journey into the innermost depths of one's own life, into the depths of Life itself.

PRAYING WITH BEADS

Any good bead or craft store can help you find the beads you need and teach you how to string them together. I encourage even the "craft challenged" to string their own prayer beads, as the process itself can be a spiritual exercise. Gather together one large bead, four medium-sized beads, twenty-three small beads, and a cord. String the beads in the following order: large bead (Centering), four small beads (warm-up), first medium bead (Naming), five small beads (breath prayer), second medium bead (Knowing), five small beads (breath prayer), third medium bead (Listening), five small beads (breath prayer), fourth medium bead (Loving), and four small beads (cool-down). Connect the cord back to the original large bead, completing the circle.

Begin to work your way through the beads, holding one at a time. Start with the largest one.

CENTERING: The large bead is for *Centering* yourself in preparation for the journey. Breathe in and out several times, calming the body and quieting the mind. You might sit quietly with your breath, recite a "breathing gatha" or chant, or sing a favorite hymn ("Spirit of Life," "Voice Still and Small," and "Find a Stillness" all work well). When you feel ready, move on.

NAMING (Prayers of Praise and Thanksgiving): The first medium-sized bead is for *Naming* the Holy. In the Islamic tradition God has ninety-nine names. There are Baha'i prayers that consist of nothing but lists of names and attributes for the Divine. The Psalms in the Hebrew Scriptures are full of ways of calling out to Yahweh. This is your chance to name the Sacred, to give voice to what you consider Holy or where you have felt the Divine in your life. You might use the names of gods and goddesses from the world's religions and you might make up your own. (I have sometimes said: "Ancient and Ageless Spirit: known in many ways, by many names and by no name at all—Holy Sanctamataba, Mother and Father of All; Gods and Goddesses of old; all Buddhas throughout space and time; Spirits, Saints, and Sages; Wise Women and Men. . . .") If you prefer not to imagine the Divine as personal, you could call up the attributes that you ascribe to the Sacred or name whatever feeds your soul; this is your opportunity to give name to what you feel to be holy and sacred. This bead is also the place for you to lift up all for which you are thankful at this moment, all the blessings and miracles in your life, all the joy in your living. Take your time. "Count your blessings" as the old phrase has it.

KNOWING (Prayer of Confession): The second medium-sized bead is for *Knowing* yourself. "Thou has searched me and known me, O my God," sang the Psalmist, yet it is at least equally important to know yourself. Here you have an opportunity to reflect on your life as it is today, to recognize those places that call for reconciliation and atonement. We are all a mixture of saint and sinner, and this stop on our journey is an opportunity to see and know yourself in all your subtle shadings. This is not a call for guilt or self-criticism but for honest self-appraisal. Unless we acknowledge our faults and failings we can do nothing about overcoming them.

LISTENING (Contemplative Prayer): The third medium-sized bead calls you to sit back and *Listen;* it is a place for revelation, not discourse. "Be still and know that I am God." Be still and listen to the Divine spark, the Buddha-nature, that is inherent in us all. You may meditate silently; gaze on an icon, statue, or mandala; or reflectively read scripture, practicing what is known as *lectio devina.*

LOVING (Intercessory Prayer): The final medium-sized bead is a reminder that a prayer practice that focuses only on the self is ultimately hollow, as is a life that is too self-centered. Here we lift up those we know (and those we don't) whose lives have pain and need. Hold them in your consciousness, bring them to your awareness. Someone once asked why people had to pray to God since God knows all things and should already know about the needs of everyone. The answer was that we do not pray so that God knows about people's needs; we pray to make sure we know.

Centering, Naming, Knowing, Listening, and Loving—this is the journey of this prayer practice. Taking the time to find a quiet place in your life, setting in the front of your awareness the Holy and Sacred miracle of life, seeing yourself within that reality as full and whole, tuning your sense to hear inner wisdom, and then turning your loving attention to the needs within and around you.

What of the small beads? A set of four small beads separates the Centering Bead from the Naming Bead. These small beads provide your entry to this journey of prayer or, if you prefer a different metaphor, a warm-up period for this spiritual exercise. Here you can honor the four directions (one per bead), take the four Boddhisattva vows, or recite a four-line poem which moves you. Four small beads also separate the Loving Bead from the Centering Bead, mirroring the first four, providing a spiritual cool-down, a chance to open the circle and thank the directions, repeat your vows, and bring yourself gently back to the everyday world.

Five small beads separate each of the medium-sized beads, providing a link between the stages of the journey. With each of these beads you may use a "breath prayer," a two-line phrase that is said in rhythm with the in- and out-breaths: for example, "Breathing in I develop calm and equanimity / Breathing out I find peace and joy"; "Lord Jesus Christ / have mercy on me"; "Great Mystery / I seek to know." Many traditions extol the virtues of repetitive, set prayers over which the practitioner has no control; this kind of praying removes any ego-involvement from the composition process, preventing you from getting caught up in eloquent or flowery phrases. Many today look down on such a practice as too formal or ritualistic, but it has great power; try it and see.

This entire prayer bead practice can take anywhere from thirty to sixty minutes. You can, of course, shorten or lengthen it depending on available time and your own sense of need. I carry my beads with me wherever I go and often find myself fingering them while on line or in a meeting. Sometimes I just Center myself; sometimes I just try to Name.

Sometimes I take a whole day to do the practice, using the medium-sized beads as break points, picking up at a later time where I'd left off. At least once a week I take the entire journey, as I believe it is important to remember that these different approaches and styles of prayer are interconnected, are part of a whole, each feeding the others.

Someone once said that wise people do not begin to sew their parachutes as they are jumping out of a plane. The same can be said of our prayer life: We ought not begin trying to pray in our time of greatest need. The phrase *spiritual practice* implies something done with regularity and intention, something we return to again and again. A related phrase—*spiritual discipline*—is not much in favor these days, because many people see in it a sense of being forced, of rigidity, of lifelessness. Yet there is much in it I think we would do well to reclaim. You can make sounds on a musical instrument playing it from time to time, whenever the mood strikes; you can learn to make music if your practice has an element of discipline.

This practice was developed with an eye toward balance—raising up what I am thankful for and what I know needs work, looking at myself and bringing to mind the needs of others, naming the holy and sacred dimensions of life as I know them and listening to what life will say to me. With its mixture of free, spontaneous prayer and set, repetitive prayer, this practice aims at providing a fully rounded experience of a life of prayer. I have found this to be an exciting way to bring disciplined prayer back into my life and have found it to be flexible enough to hold my varied spiritual influences. It is with great joy and hope that I share it with you.

ENGAGING THE BODY

Activity and Nourishment

Movement

Robert T. Hughes

I grew up with a love of books and information—so much so that I sometimes thought of myself as a "human knowing" rather than a human being! In time, though, I began to realize that I was cut off from my body. I started to search for ways to integrate body, mind, emotions, and spirit. I began taking a class in the martial arts discipline of tai chi, and since then movement has become an integral part of my spiritual practice.

Widely practiced in China, tai chi is a discipline involving slow, elegant gestures that increase the body's flexibility. (The movements are similar to patterns I have seen used in physical therapy rehabilitation programs, leading me to think they might be able to prevent injuries in healthy people as well.) Much of what I will say about tai chi is true of disciplines such as yoga and aikido as well.

Beginning a class in tai chi challenged me in several ways. The first challenge was learning the practice itself. I became conscious of how difficult it was for me to learn; I went through the beginner's class twice! I recalled feelings of awkwardness as a child: Was my lack of physical grace a result of my overemphasis on academic learning and separation from my body? I needed to find new ways of experiencing life, outside the intellectual way of learning I was used to.

Tai chi also challenged my preconceptions about everything from exercise to philosophy. The physical exercises I had done before—high school gym class, the Army "daily dozen"—had been of the "more, farther, faster" variety. In the tai chi class, however, the instructor once said, "see how slowly you can do this movement. Keep moving, don't stop, just see how *slowly* you can keep moving." This was a novel approach for me! It was a challenge to my perspective, and it felt refreshingly appropriate. The differences between tai chi's Eastern, intuitive approach and the Western, linear one with which I had grown up led me to a growing interest in exploring other paradigms.

My awareness that I was a slow learner when it came to body-based teachings was not easy, but it helped me toward a greater development of what is called the "Observer Self." This is the part of our make-up that notices what is going on around and within us, that listens to the significant messages our bodies are sending at all times. The observer self is important in tai chi, because the practice requires awareness of what is happening in one's body, especially at one's center (located about two inches below the navel). In doing the movement called "pat high horse," for example, one might become aware of stiffness in the right shoulder. What is important is simply to observe that stiffness, without judging or criticizing it.

Beginning to observe the realities of my body gave me a starting point for observing other aspects of my self. Developing and strengthening the Observer Self is a basic aspect of human transformation, enabling us to notice such things as a tendency to criticize others, a short temper, or misconceptions about the world without criticizing them. Such a compassionate approach is helpful in human growth. In fact, in their book *The Undefended Self,* Susan Thesenga and Eva Pierrakos write that "the ability to observe ourselves objectively and compassionately is the single most important skill to develop in walking the spiritual path." Starting to develop one's Observer Self in meditative movement is a fairly nonthreatening way to further one's opportunities for personal and spiritual growth.

Another benefit tai chi gave me was the lesson offered by long-term practice. Tai chi isn't "learned"; it is a process. Actually tai chi could be described as a physical manifestation of the Taoist approach to life: Neither is ever done perfectly! Before I began tai chi, my own perspective reflected my culture; I was committed to the quick fix. If I had a headache, I took an aspirin. If something hurt, I wanted the doctor to fix it quickly. Problems were to be resolved rapidly, and preferably in my favor! Participating in a practice that would never be done perfectly or mastered was novel to me. It was a concrete manifestation of the reality that not all problems are readily solved, that some things are to be lived with, and that some things take a long time. My decision to repeat the beginner's classes and realization that tai chi is a life-long process reflect the reality that the process can be as important as the product.

Tai chi has helped me in psychological, philosophical, and spiritual ways, as well as in physical ones. Tai chi asks that one be aware of one's body and center at all times. Such an awareness has given me a greater sense of balance. The repetitive movements, done in accordance with the way muscles are apparently designed to move, have enhanced my flexibility. And together, these have created a sense of grace and bodily harmony that, while imperfect, is new and delightful for me.

Finally, tai chi has opened the doors to the study of other practices integrating movement and spirituality. I regularly do the exercises that are part of "Integral Transformative Practice" (ITP), a practice developed by George Leonard and Michael Murphy that seeks to recognize and reintegrate the reality that each person is a whole entity. ITP involves a series of stretches and movements as well as aerobic exercise, diet, intellectual stimulation, and sharing goals with others. I have also found Thomas Hanna's work on somatics valuable. Hanna has developed exercises that teach the body to relearn flexible movements. After learning the somatic exercises, one may maintain flexibility through a daily Cat Stretch, and I heartily recommend doing the Cat Stretch each day.

My experiences have convinced me that reconnecting with one's body, becoming aware of the desirability of an intuitive perspective, and committing to long-term practice form a part of a spiritual discipline. To the extent that we are integrated beings—with mind, body, emotions, and spirit merely different ways of conceptualizing the self—an intentional practice such as tai chi, yoga, or aikido is a spiritual discipline. All of us have become dis-integrated and experienced the mind-body split. If re-integration is our goal, then the methods involved should include something physical as well as mental. To the extent that there is re-integration, there is healing, and the furthering of one's spiritual journey.

How can one get started on this journey? I recommend several books, tapes, and videos, listed in the resource section of this book. In addition, I suggest that you locate a teacher of tai chi or yoga near you. (One helpful distinction between the two is that tai chi has retained some of its martial arts origins, whereas yoga has no connections with fighting.)

I am convinced that it is best to learn with a teacher and in a group. Video instruction in tai chi can be helpful, but it cannot replace a human being. As you search for a teacher, remember that you are the final authority on you. As George Leonard says, you need to trust your teacher's guidance, and you need to be responsible for your own learning, not pushing your body beyond what it can safely do. (There are instances of yoga or aikido teachers, for example, who pushed students too quickly into a posture or movement and injuries resulted. I appreciate Leonard's constant admonition, "do what is safe and comfortable *for you*"—another refreshingly novel approach for many of us!)

In an arresting phrase in his *A Brief History of Everything,* philosopher Ken Wilber argues that many of our current difficulties can be traced to the Western world's failure to develop any "truly *contemplative practices.*" Wilber says that there has been "no yoga, no meditative discipline, no experimental methodology to reproduce in consciousness the transpersonal insights and intuitions of its founders (the

Idealists)." Wilbur maintains that those who emphasized human rationality failed because their system only served to "*map* the world and doesn't sufficiently provide interior technologies to change the mapmaker." I am convinced that practices such as tai chi, yoga, aikido, and ITP provide us with those experiential methodologies that are a part of our ongoing growth and transformation—our spiritual discipline. I wish you well in your own journey!

Martial Arts

Sarah Lammert

There are small lava rocks in the grass from an earlier wind-storm, in which these rocks were strewn from the roof tops all over the campus walkways and greens. My bare feet do not appreciate them, and as we proceed through our warm-up kicks and sets I occasionally yelp and throw a rock out of the way. Still, by the time we have run through some more complex movements, I am no longer aware of the rocks. I am inside my body, the muscles, tendons, and bones. And I am inside my soul.

I have been practicing martial arts for about six years—three different styles of karate and kung fu for the three different cities I have lived in during this time. I was introduced to the idea while living in Brooklyn, New York, and feeling a bit vulnerable in the big city. I read a book entitled *Women in the Martial Arts* and was amazed to discover that one of the teachers highlighted had a studio not three blocks from my apartment. I arrived the first day expecting to learn a thing or two about self-defense. Little did I know how much I would come to love this art form.

Some people enjoy prayer, meditation, yoga, tai chi—the quiet and calming ways to get centered and touch the holy within and without. While I do enjoy a small dose of such practices, what I have discovered about myself is that I much prefer kicking, screaming, and punching as a spiritual path! The martial arts for me embody the unity of heart, mind, and body. There are slow, spiral movements that look like leaves floating down into a pond; there are sharp, stinging movements that mimic fierce animals; there are powerful, sly balancing acts that require lightness and strength in the same moment. To practice the martial arts you must use your mind to memorize and to plot strategic movements. You must engage your body, which you come to rely on to be both quick and slow, balanced and strong. And you must touch a place beyond mind and body, what in Chinese is called *chi* and in Japanese is called *ki*—the center of your energy, the soul.

Before I walked into the Brooklyn Women's Martial Arts studio, I was really quite disengaged from my own body. Many women who have experienced abuse, rape, or other kinds of physical trauma report that they find it difficult to reconnect to their bodies, in some cases even feeling a sensation of floating around somewhere outside of themselves as they go through the motions of living their daily lives. While my case was not this extreme, owing to a date-rape experience in my teens I had definitely lost the ability to soak in the sunshine, to accept caresses without guard, to walk barefoot on the beach and give myself to the ocean. It was as if a part of myself had decided the best defense was to detach from my own sensuality. If I couldn't really feel my body, no one else could take it from me.

What I found in the rigorous exercise of karate was a doorway back to wholeness. Almost imperceptibly, in the company only of women, I began to heal in a deep, cellular way. As I learned to set my foot just so, bending my knees and pulling in through my abdomen to hold a pose on one leg, or practiced moving through a series of animal- or insect-like movements, I came back inside of myself again. Sometimes, class could be painful, as my muscles protested, the summer heat battered us, or I simply could not get a movement right, even after one hundred repetitions. At other times, class was pure joy, as everything came together in a harmonious flow. As I was learning the basics of punching, standing, breathing, blocking, kicking, and yelling my fierce warrior cry, I was learning the basics of being a human in a body again. I was letting go of baggage that was keeping me from my own growth as a spiritual and physical person.

The history of the martial arts stretches back over centuries, to 520 BCE. At this time, Bodhidharma, a Buddhist monk from southern India, traveled at the request of his teacher Prajnatara to China with the mission of revitalizing the practice of Buddhism. He eventually stopped at the Shaolin temple, where he found the monks in poor physical and mental condition and in fact sleeping through their meditations. He began to work with the monks, teaching them a moving meditation practice called Shih Pa Lo Han Sho, or the 18 Hands of Lo Han. These movements, developed originally by Lao Tsu, imitated the movements of insects. They were never intended to be a martial practice, but were purely to help the monks become more mentally and physically fit.

Some forty years after Bodhidharma's death, the Shaolin monastery came under a series of raids by brigands. During one of the attacks one of the monks, known only to history as the "begging monk," fought off several of the outlaws with an impressive array of hand and foot techniques, driving the brigand away. The other monks were so impressed that they asked him to teach them his method, a fighting form which he called Chuan Fa, or the Fist Way. From this time, the practice of martial arts grew at the Shaolin temple and eventually made its way across Asia. The practice came to the United States after Armed Services soldiers were introduced to the martial arts during World War II.

It is only in the last twenty-five years or so that a significant number of women have broken into the martial arts, which had formerly been reserved only for men. My women teachers have all been pioneers in the art, putting up with a lot of macho behavior along the way from the male students (and sometimes teachers) who dominated their schools. I have been lucky to study predominantly in the company of women, although my current school is roughly balanced in terms of gender.

What remains a spiritual struggle for me in practicing this art is the fact that it is a fighting method. During my most recent class I learned movements intended to blind, choke, break knees, break ribs, and generally incapacitate my opponent. Some of the movements are intended to flat out kill the opponent. So where does this leave one spiritually? At peace? In the arms of the loving One, embracing the web of life, experiencing the wonder and oneness of all being? Paradoxically, while at times I do feel unsettled by the inherent violence of such techniques, most often I am left with a greater sense of harmony and peace.

I intend no harm with my skills in fighting, but I am willing to use them if necessary for my own defense, and for those who would be harmed unjustly around me. When Jesus said to "love your enemies," I do not believe he meant to teach that love means allowing one person to destroy, dehumanize, or hurt another. Perhaps what he was really saying is that the enemy is ourselves, and that we need to embrace and love the wholeness of who we are, both good and bad, in order to be fully human. What I fear most is not the channelling of aggression in responsible ways, but its repression. No one is exempt from anger, and when stifled it too easily becomes expressed as violence, whether self-destructive, or harmful of another.

At this stage in my life, with a full-time career as a minister and a small child to take care of at home, I am not as interested in the sparring aspect of the martial arts as I once was. I'm just not up for broken ribs and noses the way I used to be! My current teacher, Lee Jones, prefers to focus solely on kata, which are choreographed movements against an imaginary opponent. Many of them appear to be elaborate, flowing dances to the untrained eye. In fact, when the peasants were prohibited from studying the martial arts in China for fear they would empower an uprising, the kata were used to disguise their continued practice. Although we do work with partners, there are virtually no injuries in my current school, which is just fine with me. I am happy that there are choices within the martial arts about the level of intensity with which to engage the practice.

When I remove my street clothes and don my black *gi,* removing my shoes and tying on my belt, I enter a different time and space. I am literally walking barefoot on holy ground, as I set aside a special time to reconnect with body, mind, and spirit. My feet have been through a lot with this unaccustomed shoelessness—blistering up, healing, and becoming callused and strong. Despite the hazards of lava rocks, twigs, and pine needles, my favorite times of the year are the spring and summer when we practice outdoors. There, the connection and energy I feel seem to run from the sky and from the earth, literally infusing me with vibrancy and life. As I bow out at the end of class, I re-enter the world, calmer, more grounded, and at peace.

Yoga

Eva S. Hochgraf

No matter how busy I am, every day I do yoga. I do it even if I'm very busy, or on vacation, because I just don't feel right if I don't. It's not just that yoga helps my back feel less achy, and keeps my shoulders straighter; it helps me start out my day feeling calm and centered. For me, yoga is a kind of living, moving meditation. As I do the series of poses, my mind settles down, and I reach a point of clarity and focus that carries though my day.

Yoga, developed in India, is a series of postures coordinated with breathing techniques, an exercise that helps make muscles strong and flexible. I've been doing it off and on for most of my life. My first yoga class was part of an experimental Sunday school course offered to people of all ages. I remember learning about slow, deep breathing there—a skill best learned early in life. I wowed the grown-ups in the class with my flexibility—imagine actually being better at something than grown-ups! And I learned some basic stretches and poses that I used time and again as I later rode horses, played soccer and racquetball, and rode bicycles. Yoga kept me flexible and made a great warm-up. It also taught me a basic respect for my body, which kept me aware of the deep relationship between the body and the mind.

I didn't take another class, though, until after my first baby was born. The rhythm of parenting was very unfamiliar, and the wear and tear on my body from carrying the baby was very noticeable. I felt out of sorts, out of shape, and far too achy to exercise. When I began the yoga class, I was shocked at how stiff and inflexible I was; even the simple poses seemed challenging. But even more shocking was the fact that it took just a few weeks, with only occasional home practice, to get from sitting on the floor, barely able to touch my toes, to nearly touching my head to my knee!

Somewhere along the way, I began to notice how much of a calming effect yoga had on me, an effect that lasted even when I went home to a trying two-year-old. As my body stretched out and my muscles had a chance to quit being so tense, my mind followed.

MY PRACTICE

Every morning, before I get up, I like to start my day with a few deep breaths. It wakes me up, and reminds me to start the day in a deliberately calm way. I do a few simple poses in bed to help get my blood flowing. It's easy to bring your leg over to the other side of your body as you lie on your back and allow your spine to feel a gentle twist. Some mornings I start with a gentle rocking of the hips to wiggle out the kinks. It doesn't have to be very big or dramatic; it can be whatever comes to mind. What is most important is to enter the day with a body awareness.

I like to do my regular routine before breakfast; yoga's not fun on a full stomach! Because some mornings are very hectic while others afford me a bit more time, I like to do a routine that has a lot of possibilities for leisurely expansion or hasty contraction. A daily routine must be flexible enough to meet the demands of my schedule, yet routine enough to do without much thought. I find yoga, like most of life, is most satisfying when it reaches that comfortable balance between adaptability and habit.

So I usually do a yoga series, like the Sun Salutation or the Moon Salutation, for my bare-bones minimum. Be-

cause we do these series frequently in class, I don't have
to think about what comes next. I also know how to play
with them, to add poses or refine moves when I have time.
These series work particularly well when they are repeated,
once on the busy days, a few more times when I'm in the
mood. Even if I do them just once, though, I feel the difference as I head out the door—my head held high, my
steps light and limber.

GETTING STARTED

If you want to start doing yoga, you can begin either by
taking a class or by learning from a book or video. But it
would be best to begin with a class, because it's much easier
to copy a person than a picture and to have a teacher to
answer your questions. There is also something to be said
for keeping your momentum going by attending the class. It
just seems to be easier to set aside time to go to a class than
time for regular practice at home.

The decision to begin with a class is not entirely your
own, however, because some communities are gifted with
many yoga class options and others have few or none. If
you're not sure which of these categories you're in, try searching for a class at the local YMCA or YWCA, parks and rec-
reation program, or community college. Or look for ads in
your local freebie paper. If you can't find a class that's conve-
nient, don't just throw in the towel. You can still learn a lot
and experience the benefits of yoga through books and videos.
I would recommend looking through a copy of *Yoga Journal*
for many resources to begin your home practice. Your local
library may have some resources you can explore as well.

However, you may find so many different classes that you
don't know where to begin. I suggest that you look first for
a teacher who has some training and experience and a class
that is offered at a good time and place for you. That being
said, there really are many different kinds of yoga. Some,
like hatha yoga, are very exercise oriented. Some, like

Kundalini yoga, are much more energy focused. Iyengar yoga is very precise and very helpful in realigning your posture and balance.

Yoga classes can also be very different from each other. Some yoga classes include individual poses, often increasing in difficulty throughout the class time, while others will run through a specific series of poses every time. Some yoga uses a lot of props, while others need nothing more than a mat. Some will do poses to music, some are aerobic, and most will offer a time of relaxation at the end. You will need to experiment until you find the class that is right for you. Ask to try a beginning class for one time before committing to a whole session. If you'd like to expand your horizons beyond the particular class you're in, take yoga workshops or go to retreats. Ask your teacher for referrals.

As you become a yoga practitioner, you will learn that yoga is much more than an odd kind of exercise; it is much more spiritual and metaphysical than limber limbs. Its Indian roots give a deep sense of philosophy. What we in the Western world call yoga is really just an athletic branch of the total idea of yoga as it is classically understood in India. Yoga includes branches that focus on the ideas of nonviolence, selfless service, vegetarianism, breath and energy pathways, meditation, chanting, prayer, self-inquiry, and more. Yoga is a total life philosophy that offers rich rewards at whatever level you encounter it.

FOR YOUR REFERENCE

Here are some of the most popular schools of yoga with simple descriptions to help you decide where to begin.

Ashtanga yoga: Vigorous and athletic, this form of yoga, popularized by K. Pattabhi Jois, stretches and strengthens the body by moving rapidly through one of several series of challenging poses.

Integral yoga: Meditative and devotional, this form of yoga, developed by Swami Satchidananda, incorporates all of the traditional branches of yoga (chanting, meditation, breath, etc.).

Ishta yoga: Athletic and esoteric, this form of yoga, developed by Mani Finger and popularized in New York and Los Angeles by his son Alan, focuses on opening subtle energy channels through postures, guided meditation, and guided visualization.

Iyengar yoga: Precise and focused, this form of yoga, founded by B. K. S. Iyengar, uses props and careful instruction to draw your attention to alignment and refinement of each pose.

Kripalu yoga: Introspective and soft, this form of yoga, developed by Yogi Amrit Desai, uses prolonged holding of postures to explore and release spiritual and emotional blockages in a noncompetitive and loving atmosphere.

Kundalini yoga: Energetic and contemplative, this form of yoga, popularized by the Sikh Guru Yogi Bhajan, concentrates on awakening the subtle energy that lies dormant at the base of the spine and drawing it upward through each of the seven chakras using chanting, breath exercises, meditation, as well as a series of postures.

Sivananda yoga: Similar to integral yoga, this form of yoga, founded by Swami Vishnudevananda and popularized by yoga instructor Lilias Folan on PBS, combines the many branches of yoga to emphasize healthy and balanced living.

Tri yoga: Dance-like and creative, this form of yoga was developed by Kali Ray and uses music to move to a series of postures followed by breath exercises and meditation.

Vini yoga: Contemplative and gentle, this form of yoga, founded by T. K. V. Desikarachar, offers sequences of poses synchronized with the breath.

Exercise

Scott W. Alexander

Every day, almost without exception, I take an hour to tend my relationship with my oldest and most intimate friend—my body. Noon is my favorite time to lace up a pair of running shoes, do a little stretching, and step outside—regardless of weather—for a good, swift run.

This daily practice is almost always the most enjoyable part of my day. I love the expansive freedom of this time outdoors. As I run, I love noticing the pleasing intricacies and healing grace of both natural and human worlds: sunlight kissing a passing cloud, a cormorant gracefully diving for a fish, children recklessly playing in the sand. I love the experience of feeling so physically present and alive. And I love the feeling when I have finished—that glow of both accomplishment and invigoration—that enables me to return to my day with my body refreshed, my mind reawakened, my soul rejuvenated. Exercise enables me to meet the duties and demands of my day relaxed, focused, alert, patient, and eager.

Everyone knows that regular, vigorous exercise offers a wide constellation of health benefits, as well as a general enhancement of personal well-being and enjoyment of life. But what makes it a *spiritual* practice? Isn't that—pardon the pun—stretching it a bit? I think not. A spiritual practice is any regular, intentional activity that serves to significantly deepen the quality and content of your relationship with the miracle of life. For me, running is a spiritual practice that connects me in deep, satisfying, and enriching ways with myself, other people, my world, and the day.

The spiritual aspects of exercise are twofold. First, exercise has meditative and reflective dimensions. Many who exercise regularly report that their physical discipline helps them to achieve a state of mindful and meditative peace and calm. If I relax while running—focus my mind on the regular rhythms of both my breathing and body movements, and let go of the distractions and complexities of my day—I often move into a spiritual state of being fully alive to the rich miracle of life both within and around me. I feel in soul-satisfying harmony with all that is: my body, the natural world, other people, even what I call God. While running does not always bring me to this calming, meditative place, regular exercise can often be a time to meditate, to become more aware of and grateful for life.

Second, I believe that the regular practice of physical exercise is crucial for establishing an overall spiritual "right relation" with myself, my world, and other human beings who share it with me. I believe that if I care for the body that houses and holds me, I will be more inclined and more able to care for other lives around me. Paul of Tarsus, in his first letter to the Corinthians (6:19-20), similarly affirmed the spiritual value of good self-care by way of a spiritual question and statement, "Or do you not know that your body is a temple of the Holy spirit within you, which you have from God . . . therefore glorify God in your body."

So taking responsible care of your own bodily temple can properly be seen as a primary spiritual practice—a spiritual practice of connection and care that leads to caring connections with other human beings and the infinite intricacies of the wider world. Any form of regular, vigorous exercise that you both enjoy and are physically capable of doing at this point in your life can be a discipline of spiritual self-care that naturally leads to spiritual other-care, and thus to right relation with all you encounter and touch.

But regular exercise is, for many of us, easier said than done. The U.S. Public Health Service reports that only 20 percent of Americans regularly exercise enough to achieve any cardiovascular benefit. How, in a culture that prides itself on rationality and good health care practices, have we come to neglect the exercise we know our bodies (and souls) need? The answer, I suggest, is as much philosophical as it is physical. I believe that the centuries-old philosophy of Cartesian dualism has allowed us to distance ourselves from, and thus dangerously disregard, our own physical bodies.

First postulated by ancient Greek philosophers like Plato and Aristotle, Cartesian dualism postulates an absolute dichotomy between the physical/fleshy/material realm (which was philosophically devalued because of its temporal and common earthiness) and the realm of mind/spirit/intellect (which was valued much more highly). Descartes, for whom the phrase *Cartesian dualism* was named, and many other post-Hellenistic philosophers accepted this divided worldview, and continued to suggest that the spiritual/mental world can and should be judged superior to the physical one.

Today such fiercely dualistic thinking continues to permeate much of Western thought, and our often-unconscious acceptance of this worldview encourages us to devalue and neglect many things we deem merely physical—including our bodies and the earth itself. So many of us in this culture continue to treat our bodies as if they are auxiliary things, somehow separate and disconnected from the so-called higher realities of mind and spirit that make us fully human.

I believe, on the contrary, that human wholeness and health are impossible if we separate the spiritual from the physical in our lives. All of life is woven together in an interdependent web of connection and relationship. If we do not nurture, tend, and care for our bodies, we will not succeed in maintaining a proper and lively spiritual relationship with ourselves, our neighbors, our earth, and the holistic mystery that is being itself. My friend Edward Frost writes, "Having survived a heart attack and a quadruple bypass, I decided

I'd like to go on living. I began to exercise regularly, three times a week at the club. I hated every minute of it. My mind dragged my body to the club. Now, however, my exercising is an everyday, deeply spiritual whole-person experience—not something I do simply to stay alive, but a profoundly satisfying part of my life." Regular physical exercise appropriate to your physical condition and age is a profoundly necessary—and usually, with time, extremely rewarding—practice. Exercising your body is not something to do if and when you can find the time, but a fundamental necessity that makes you healthy, whole, and fully alive.

GETTING STARTED

Once you have truly resolved to regularly exercise your body, the first thing you must do is to refuse to allow yourself not to do it. The most frequently used excuse is, "I just don't have time," but we must make time, disciplining ourselves to set it aside on a regular, faithful basis. Remember, this is of paramount importance because you're not just seeking physical fitness but spiritual wholeness itself.

The second thing to do is to begin slowly and appropriately given your physical condition, age, body type, and personal exercise preferences. People often make grand (and unrealistic) resolutions about beginning an exercise regimen, only to quit days later (in frustration and shame) because their plans were either too extravagant or demanding. Plan on building up your exercise routine gradually, to allow both your body and personal schedule to adjust to these new demands (and, I promise you, delights!). Not everyone is going to run a marathon, swim the English Channel, or become a prize-winning weight lifter—you may do far, far less on your way to achieving appropriate physical fitness and balance for your life and body. So be sensible and patient, but stick with it!

Third, before you begin any new exercise regimen (whether you are out of shape or not) please see your phy-

sician to ensure that your body is ready f
you are planning.

The variety of exercise forms and pr
you is wide and welcoming. The key is b
are; always being respectful of (and nonanxious a_
physical limitations, age, and personal preferences; and neve.
allowing yourself to fall back into inactivity. Again I must
warn you: The ready excuses *not* to exercise regularly (with
discipline and duty) are virtually infinite and conveniently
persuasive! My regular exercise routine helps me stay in
healthy right relation—with myself, nature, other persons,
indeed all of existence itself—and allows me to feel truly at
home in my body and in the world. In the end, that familiar
athletic shoe company slogan had it right. "JUST DO IT!"

Fasting

Marta Morris Flanagan

I want to fast to help me
slow down and connect with myself,
to be more conscious of my decisions,
not only about food, but about all the ways
that I "stuff" my feelings, my spirit.
I want to live more consciously.
— Matt Muise
member, First Universalist Church
Salem, Massachusetts

The fast would begin in the company of others. For three years, I invited members of the Universalist Church in Salem, Massachusetts, to join me in a three-day juice fast during the week before Easter. We would begin Monday evening and break the fast following the congregation's customary Maundy Thursday evening service. Each year more than a dozen people fasted.

We would begin with music, silent meditation, and sharing. We listened to music from the Weston Priory, chants from the Shakers, bluegrass music by Alison Krauss, and arias by Bach. We would speak of what we expected or wanted to happen during the fast.

We would read from Thich Nhat Hanh. This Buddhist monk writes of giving tangerines to children. The children take a tangerine in the palm of their hand. As they look at the tangerine they are asked to meditate on the origins of the tangerine. They see the tangerine and its mother, the tangerine tree. They visualize tangerine blossoms in the sunshine and in the rain. They see petals falling down and the tiny green fruit appears. The tangerine grows, someone picks it, and then it arrives in the palm of their hand. The children peel the tangerine slowly, noticing its mist and fragrance. They bring it to their mouths and have a mindful bite, aware of its texture and taste of its juice. They eat slowly. They see deeply into the tangerine. They see the universe in one tangerine. They take time eating the tangerine and are happy.

After the reading by Thich Nhat Hanh, one of us would take an apple and cut it in silence. We would listen to the sound of the knife splitting open the apple. A plate of apple slices would be passed among us. Slowly, mindfully, each would smell, taste, and eat a single apple slice in silence. It would be the last thing we would eat for the next three days.

I began fasting as the minister of the Universalist Church in Salem. Now, as one of the co-ministers at the Unitarian Universalist Church in Portsmouth, New Hampshire, I join the Youth Group in their fast as they contemplate world hunger. I also welcome occasions for fasting with members of the congregation just as I did in Salem.

I fast at least once a year, for three days at a time. I abstain from all solid food and limit myself to drinking fruit juices, herbal tea, and water. This juice fast prevents dehydration and provides many vital nutrients while still inviting me to abstain and feel that emptiness of body and openness of soul.

When I fast, I pay greater attention to life. I am more mindful. Some practice fasting as a time of repentance and self-sacrifice. For them, like other ascetic practices, fasting involves the denial or withholding of pleasure. But for me, fasting is not a form of suffering, because I do not find suffering in and of itself a useful spiritual discipline.

Instead, I fast to make more room for God. When I want to deepen or reawaken my sense of the Spirit, it is helpful to let go of something else. When I fast, I create more room for

God in my life, sometimes simply by the large amount of time that is freed from thinking about, shopping for, and preparing food. My hunger during the fast also serves as a visceral reminder of my own deepest yearnings.

We are all hungry people. It is often difficult to be in touch with our spiritual hunger if we are satiated with food. Try to meditate on a full stomach! Often we stuff ourselves with food in a vain attempt to feed another kind of hunger that cannot be satisfied with food. Often we fill our hungers with food, with drink, with busyness, with distractions like television. Fasting is a time-honored spiritual discipline that awakens us to the deeper hungers within.

During a fast we give up anything that has become a habit that might harm the body during the fasting period: caffeine, nicotine, alcohol, sweeteners of all kinds, coffee, drugs, and medicines, as far as possible. Fasting is not appropriate for people who battle bulimia or anorexia or those with special health problems. But fasting for a short period of time is healthy for most others. It cleanses the body of toxins. Some medical doctors have advocated fasting for purely physical health reasons. I find that the first twenty-four hours are the hardest physically. I can feel tired and have headaches. But there is a sense of freedom that comes to me on the second day.

In the beginning of a fast many people are fascinated by the physical aspects of the experience. But more important is to monitor the attitude of your heart.

Fasting is spiritual discipline known to every world religion. The Jewish calendar includes several fast days, most prominently the Day of Atonement or Yom Kippur, while Muslims fast between dawn and dusk during the month of Ramadan. In the Christian tradition, fasting was once a common discipline, continuing from the early church up to the Reformation. During the Middle Ages, it became associated with excessive ascetic practices involving rigid regulations and extreme self-mortification and thus fell into disfavor. In recent years, fasting has attracted renewed interest.

Moses, David, Zoroaster, Confucius, Plato, Socrates, Aristotle, and Buddha all fasted for spiritual reasons. Like Elijah, who was fasting when he heard a still small voice, we are more open to the Spirit when we fast. And like Jesus, who was fasting when he was tested in the wilderness, we realize depths of faith and personal powers when we fast.

Why fast?

Fasting reveals things that control us. We often cover up what is inside us with food. When we fast, these things surface. While fasting we may feel the sorrow, anger, regret, or pride we have been hiding from ourselves.

Fasting is a way to bring awareness to what we do. Many of us eat for emotional comfort. It becomes an automatic impulse.

Fasting helps us pay attention, and when we do, our relationship to things changes. We see more and see more deeply. We are present to the moment.

Fasting helps us return to a balance in our lives. How easily we let the nonessential take precedence. How quickly we crave things we do not need.

Fasting is a time to write in a journal, pray, meditate, walk. These are all ways of being receptive to grace.

When fasting, it is helpful to keep daily concerns and distractions to a minimum. I do not watch television when I fast. Instead of relying on stimuli from the outside, it's best to try living with yourself. Let yourself be directed from within.

When fasting, do whatever does your body good. If you are tired, sleep. If you like physical activity, exercise. Do things that please you: Read, dance, or listen to music.

When you fast it is helpful to reflect each day. Ask yourself:

- What was hardest about today's fast? What was easiest?
- What surprised me about fasting today?
- In what ways did I become aware of the deeper hunger of my soul today?

- What were the inner demons I encountered today on this fast?
- What special grace did I experience today?

You may give your fast a focus. Some people are mindful that two-thirds of the world go hungry every day. They fast as an act of concern and identification. The money saved from this experience goes toward hunger. I know of one person who was so struck by an insight into himself during a therapy session that he spontaneously observed a twenty-four-hour fast to help him remember and deepen that insight.

Beginning and ending a fast is important. At the Universalist Church in Salem, we broke our three-day fast by gathering for a meditative service similar to the one that began the fast. Each participant would bring a reading, a poem, or a passage that spoke to us during the fast. Everyone would also bring a piece of fruit.

Silently, one by one, we'd approach the table and prepare our piece of fruit and place the pieces on china plates—one for each participant. One person would slowly cut a banana and place the slices on each plate. Another person would peel and divide the sections of an orange; the aroma of the moist spray of the orange would fill the hungry air. Another would take blackberries and place a few berries on each plate.

When everyone had gone forward in silence and prepared their fruit, we were left with a plate for each of us with an array of fruit. It was a wondrous offering of food. Slowly, mindfully, and with great intention, we would break the fast by tasting the fruit before us. And always after the silence of our meditation, there would be laughter as we ate together. It would be good.

Mealtime

Aaron R. Payson

"Consume less—share more" touts a bumper sticker I ran across recently—a simple message with profound implications for a culture that seems to be perpetually in motion. After I graduated from theological school and got married, I, too, became a part of the rushing crowd. I was accustomed to eating pizza at midnight as I studied for exams or grabbing a sandwich between classes. During the first year or so of my ministry and my marriage, I operated in much the same way. Meals were a grab-them-when-you-can, if-you-can prospect. Sitting down to eat was a novelty.

I was not unique. Many families struggle to juggle competing work schedules, school activities, and community commitments; they lament, as they exit the drive-thru, that it is difficult, if nearly impossible, to find time to sit down to share a meal together. Yet taking time to eat together can be one of the most important activities that families do. I characterize mealtime as a spiritual discipline, an activity through which those gathered may discover depth and meaning in their lives.

It is an intriguing paradox. Researchers indicate that Americans are increasingly health conscious, decreasing fat intake and increasing consumption of high-fiber products. And many people are beginning to learn the benefits of stabilizing blood sugar levels by creating a daily routine that allows for eating less more often. As a society we have yet, however, to face another important factor affecting our diet and consequently our health: The speed with which we attempt to complete our lives and complete our meals ultimately hampers our experience of eating itself. Recent polls substantiate this, showing that between 1977 and 1987 the percentage of families eating supper together dropped from 82 percent to 65 percent. And as of 1987, 25 percent of families never ate breakfast or lunch together. I realized one night, as I ate yet another cheese steak alone at the desk in my office, that I had become part of these statistics. Right then, I decided to put a stop to all the eating on the fly. It wasn't easy to change after seven years spent diligently honing bad habits, but I had the advantage of lessons I had learned as a child and young adult when I gathered with my family around the dinner table.

GRACE

In his book *Nourishing Wisdom,* Marc David writes, "Be there when you eat. Achieve the fullest experience of your food. Taste it. Savor it. Pay attention to it. Rejoice in it." Eating is a sacred act, which is why, in most religious traditions, mealtime is made distinct from other activities by beginning with a time of grace or blessing so that those gathered to partake of the sustenance before them might be mindful of their connections to each other, to the environment, and to that which is holy around and within them.

Consider the reflections offered up by some Zen monks prior to eating a meal in silence. "I reflect on the work of others, which brings this food to me. I reflect on my imperfections and on whether I am deserving of this food. I take this food as a medicine to keep my body in good health. I accept this food so that I will fulfill my task of enlightenment." In the home of my youth, we often began dinner with a grace attributed to Johnny Appleseed, singing as we held hands around the table,

The Lord is good to me
and so I thank the Lord

for giving me
the things I need—
the sun and the rain and the apple seed. The Lord is good
    to me.

This sense of gratitude for the things that truly sustain us, of connections not only to the food but also to the elements that create and comprise it and consequently us, is the core of grace offered at mealtime. A rabbi with whom I studied once remarked that the fundamental difference between human beings and the rest of the animal kingdom is that we are capable of showing gratitude for the things that sustain us, suggesting that grace at mealtime was a ritual awakening to this reality and a reminder of our unique capacity as a species.

But grace is more than just an offering or ritual beginning to a meal. Grace is a perpetual state of awareness. Like the Zen master who teaches his disciples to eat an orange one piece at a time, learning to decrease the rate at which I eat and increase my awareness of what I am eating helps me reconnect with the source of that sustenance. I was a typical, growing teen, ravenously hungry; almost nightly, my mother paraphrased the Zen lesson for me as I inhaled my food. "I can get you a trough, you know. Slow down! No one is going to take your food away from you." Inevitably, such admonishments helped to remind me what a privilege it was to be provided with such sustenance when others, as I would come to understand, went without.

My mother had a unique way of driving such realities home by turning our times together into an opportunity for reflection and thanksgiving. Holiday meals proved most creative. At one particular Thanksgiving meal, we arrived at the dining room table, which was resplendent with our best china and crystal, to discover five single kernels of corn on each person's plate. We sat down, and Mother began, "It is said that when the pilgrims gathered at the first Thanksgiving table, each person was given just five kernels of corn, for that is all that they had to share." This was quite different from the images in most children's books, which depict a lavish meal of roast wild turkey and other game.

Mother continued, "So now we take this opportunity to share with each other five things for which we are thankful this year." This was not quite what we had expected, and I remember scrambling when my turn came. I remember being thankful for a new bike and for roller skates, for my new friend Jimmy, and yes, even for my little brother. But the next year, and the next, and the one after that, became more important; as I grew, this ritual began to take on significance. "I am thankful for the health of my family, for the opportunity to be together in the spirit of love, and for the gift of food." Consume less—share more.

NO-THANK-YOU HELPINGS

Perpetual awareness—this idea extends beyond the food itself to include reverence for the creative energy of those who prepare it. In my parents' home, the outward symbol of this reverence came in the form of no-thank-you helpings, the small portions of each food prepared that I was required to eat even if I did not particularly like them. The rationale behind this ritual was that it was a privilege to have a variety of foods to eat, much more than a choice. Indeed, it was an honor to have someone in my life who cared enough about me to prepare my food. Taking a no-thank-you helping was a way to express thanks for the privilege of having food and the honor of being served.

SETTING A PLACE FOR JUST ONE MORE

During the annual celebration of Pesach, or Passover, families and communities celebrate their journey out of the bondage of Egyptian slavery into the promised land. As the table is set with the elements of the ritual Seder meal, a place is set for the prophet Elijah, who, during the course of the meal, is welcomed into the room and invited to the table, where a glass of wine is poured for him. It was common practice for my mother to set an extra place at the table each night. On some nights it went unused, and we thought about those whom we missed at our table. On many nights, however, by the time the food was on the table, the place had been filled, either by an unexpected friend my brother or I brought home or by the person who just stopped by for a moment to chat with my father, who was a minister.

Whatever the circumstances, the guest was welcomed warmly and food was passed around. On most evenings, the atmosphere was charged with excitement, all of us chattering about the day's events. I never found it odd that guests were intrigued by the atmosphere, but I did sometimes wonder about the frequency with which certain guests arrived just at the dinner hour.

This atmosphere of celebration usually centered around the question, "What new thing did you learn today?" Author and lecturer Leo Buscaglia made this question famous. Many have heard or read about his family's rush to the encyclopedia to find something new to present at the dinner table. At our house, each of us took a moment to describe something new or something that he or she had discovered as a blessing that day. Arguments and heated discussions were not acceptable at the dinner table. Father warned us that such behavior did bad things to one's digestive tract. Whether this was true or not, this covenant made our mealtime something most of my brother's and my peers talked about for a week once they had joined us for dinner.

Father also encouraged us to think of those people in our lives who did not have family with whom they could share special meals; he always had us invite them to the table at holiday time. It was not uncommon for holiday dinners to include as many as five guests at the table, not to mention the extra place setting that was often filled by the time the meal was over. Widows from the congregation my father served, friends who lived alone, someone recently discharged from the rehabilitation unit of the hospital down the street, friends whose family did not celebrate holidays—all were welcome at the table. In a time when so much of our consumption as a culture is done on the run, mealtime has become less and less an opportunity for sharing, much less embodying an ethic of hospitality. Perhaps we still have much to learn from our brothers and sisters in the third world, who still understand that being invited to a stranger's table and learning to receive the gift of food often mean the difference between life and death.

COUPONS

Growing up as a minister's son afforded me many great opportunities to learn about life and the art of a ministry of sharing. Though I cannot say that we were ever financially rich, we were a family rich in internal resources, and we rarely went without. There were those slim times however, when there was not enough money to purchase the perfect gift or to buy the elements for a grand meal.

On such occasions, Mother once again reminded us of the power and true nature of gift-giving. Father once remarked to a group of congregants that prayer was the most creative thing we can do as sentient beings and that the most creative prayers offered for someone else are those in which we envision them as healthy and whole, doing things that make them happy. Mother actualized Father's concept of prayer in a practical way: with coupons. During slim times, when money was tight, Mother made each of us a book of coupons:

> This coupon is good for a favorite meal of your choice (48 hours' notice required).
> This coupon is good for a new pair of sneakers next month.
> This coupon entitles you to a breakfast in bed.
> This coupon entitles you to a hug whenever you need it and an ear to listen when times are hard.

This coupon entitles you to uninterrupted time to do anything you want (just give me a few minutes to put things
away).
The bearer of this coupon is loved by his family.

There were pizza parties and new clothes in spring, school
supplies, and once even a horse! The amazing part of this
ritual is that it became one of the most important mainstays
in my family's life. Often the most prized gift we received
throughout the year was a coupon.

CREATING THE PERFECT APPLE PIE

Saturday night meant an inevitable sermon block for my
father. But he had a unique ritual to clear his mind. Removing all his sermon-writing material from the kitchen table,
he would get out his baking sheet, break out the mixer, and
then prepare all the ingredients for an incredible French apple
pie. Making the pie took about an hour, and once he was
done and had placed it lovingly in the oven, he would spread
out his materials again and return to his sermon. His writer's
block would be gone, vanished in flashes of insight gained
while rolling pie crust, peeling apples. He would finish the
sermon in time to remove the piping hot pie from the oven
and place it on a cooling rack on top of the dishwasher for
a few hours. I must admit that Sunday morning breakfast
was immeasurably enhanced by the fruits of his labors.
   "Where'd the pie go?" asked Father.
   "I don't know," my brother and I would mumble, wiping the crumbs from our chin and smirking to each other.
Father would just smile and quip something pithy as he ex-
ited the room.
   Father's cure for sermon block embodies an important
lesson: The value is not necessarily in the product of one's
labor; rather, the value often lies in the process of laboring.
So too is this true at mealtime, when the ingestion of food is
only a minuscule portion of what it means to take in suste-

nance. Reclaiming mealtime is a spiritual discipline when we remember the depth of our own connections to others, to the earth and the elements that help us to grow, and to the divine spark within each of us that ignites around good company and is aflame through the presence of love that is also the substance or grace.

As I strove to make the lessons of my youth a part of my adult life, I realized that if I just slowed down, breathed a little, I was already ahead of the game. Saying grace wasn't so hard. I was and am grateful for many things. Sermon block could be staved off with many baked goods, not just apple pie. I didn't have to buy my wife expensive gifts to make her happy: A coupon for a back rub was greeted with delight, a coupon for a clean kitchen with ecstasy. As I had discovered many times as a child, a no-thank-you portion could lead to a new favorite food (I thought I didn't like oysters, until I tried my wife's oyster stew).

It was a healthy spirituality that grew our latest New Year's dinner from an intimate gathering of six to an even more intimate fifteen. With highchairs at both ends of the table and all our china service for twelve, plus three more, in use, we delightedly took our time, getting to know each other, passing around the garlic mashed potatoes, and enjoying ourselves. And yes, we said grace. And we talked of new things we had learned over the past year. And yes, we were too full to have dessert right away. But that gave us an excuse to linger over coffee, just to make room for pumpkin pie and apple crisp.

ENGAGING THE HEART

Relationship

Everyday Relationships

Jane Ellen Mauldin

When I was a teenager trying to figure out the meaning of life, I hoped that after I finished high school and college, I would finally be able to delve deeply into the meaning of things. I didn't have the language for it at that time, but I was hoping that once I was an adult, I would have the time and energy to develop a spiritual practice. Surely, in adulthood, with all of my growing up behind me, I'd be able to nurture regular habits of prayer, meditation, and study that would lead to inner calm, understanding, even enlightenment.

My expectation was bolstered in college when I read about the four life stages of a Hindu practitioner. First, student. The young person studies for what lies ahead. Second, householder. The young adult marries and raises children in short order. Third, mystic. With family responsibilities out of the way, the adult can get down to the business of studying philosophy and pondering great mysteries. Fourth, wise elder. Whether in a forest retreat or a monastery, one can live in freedom and peace and prepare for the release of death. As a young adult, I could hardly wait for that third stage, a time I imagined as leisurely meditation and heightened awareness. Surely, that time was just around the corner!

Not a chance. My route to enlightenment took a big detour into family responsibilities. After postponing childbearing until well into my thirties, I seem to have just begun the householder stage. I am so busy making school lunches, doing laundry, and driving to boy scouts and dance lessons (while

working full time, outside the home, too) that my longed-
for hour of daily meditation is still just a pipe dream. And
that's likely to be the case for a long, long time, perhaps
even for the rest of my life.

So, where's the spiritual practice for all of us household-
ers, we whose lives are filled with caring for other people?
With much trial and error, I've attempted to develop a spiritual practice of everyday relationships, to satisfy my hunger
for spiritual growth in the relationships to which I'm deeply
committed. At this time, my method has four parts that work
for me. I hope it will be a useful starting point for your own
spiritual practice.

AWARENESS

We begin with Awareness. It's easy to gulp down the coffee
in the morning with a quick look at the newspaper and an
almost peremptory "howdy" to your partner or spouse
across the table. This doesn't qualify as awareness! Take a
long look at your sweetie, at least once before you or they
run out the door. Do the same for the other people you care
for—your parent, or child, or even yourself. Really look at
these people. Know that they are there. Know that you are
near them.

Sometimes, if we are really lucky, we will get the added
benefit of our loved one's awareness, too. I was barreling
down the highway in my minivan not long ago, five minutes
late as always. Suddenly, my twelve-year-old beside me
stopped humming along to the radio and burst out: "Look,
mom!" He pointed to the sky above us. The setting sun,
behind a cloud, was streaming radiant pink, blue, and gold
rays of light in every direction. The color filled the sky as if
the sun, behind the cloud, had intensified its usual brilliance
tenfold. "Oh, mom," said my awed son, "I don't think I
will ever forget this!" His awareness focused mine. I don't
think that I will ever forget it, either.

APPRECIATION

Appreciate the present moment. For some moments, with some people, this may sound hard or even impossible. But anyone who has ever lived with a baby knows that they are very good at calling us to live in the present moment. Anyone who has cared for an ill family member, or a parent fading with Alzheimer's, knows that the present moment is very precious and is truly the only reality we have. Now. Here. If we rush through the task of wiping, feeding, assisting, then we miss the moment and we miss being alive during that time.

I was reminded to appreciate the present moment not long ago during a rainy winter morning at the doctor's office. In the bright waiting room, ancient issues of *Field and Stream* and *Woman's Day* waved from the wall. A television set blared forth a special on raising an only child (a program no longer relevant to my life), interspersed with ads for Excedrin. Near the other end of the room, audio speakers offered "lite rock" and traffic reports. My young children begged to read books and chew on them, respectively. They coughed enticingly into my face ("Here, Mom, if you don't have enough germs already, you can share mine!"). In the middle of all this hubbub, I sat overstimulated, anxious, waiting. I do not like to wait. I prefer to be going, running, driving, typing, ACCOMPLISHING, for Pete's sake. Yet there I sat, waiting.

As I fretted, I finally decided that there had to be a lesson for me, there, and it had to be something about living in the moment. As I sat on the vinyl waiting room chair, sneezing, blowing, and wiping runny noses, I knew I would rather not be there at all. But I tried to remember, anyway: What was it that I read from the Gnostic Gospel of Thomas not long ago? Jesus is reported to have said, "Split the wood and you shall find me. Lift the stone and there I am." In other words, the holiness of life can be found in damp, moist, oozy, natural places, too.

Well, my family, like so many, has damp, moist, and oozy down pretty well. Seeing the holy in relationships of caring, whether in doctors' offices or in our bedrooms, can often be a challenge. It's much easier to see the sacred in the stars at night or in the emotion of a great Sunday service. But how about in your most damp and oozy moments, even at times filled with Excedrin TV and sinus headaches? There. If we can find it there, it ought to be easy the rest of the time.

DETACHMENT FROM ATTACHMENT

Detachment from attachment is step three. Many regular spiritual practices help us wean ourselves from attachment to transitory, material things. A spiritual practice of every-day relationships does this quite well! For example, I am very attached to my expert idea of what kind of person I want my husband to be. He ought to think like me, act like me, and always come to the same logical conclusions that I do. I am, of course, often disappointed. When I expect my husband to live up to my ideal of him, I get a pretty good understanding of the Buddhist axiom that attachment is the source of suffering. If we keep hoping that reality and real people will fit our idealized standards, we will always be disappointed. Can I let go of my attachment to what I want my husband to be and do? If I can, I might be able to head down the path of unconditional love. And unconditional love—compassion, without expectations or attachment—is, many teachers say, both the source and the result of real spiritual growth.

COMMITMENT

The fourth step could also be the first step: Commitment. Yes, things and people are always changing. No, committing yourself to an abusive situation is not what I'm suggesting. Yet consider this: Every spiritual practice will have pit-falls, challenges, disappointment, pain, sleepless nights, and exhausting days. We will not grow, deepen, and achieve greater knowledge and understanding unless we are willing to make a commitment that will last us through great difficulties. At the same time that we detach ourselves from our expectations of what we want our loved one to be and do, we can also commit to loving that person and being there for him or her, no matter what (note: see above disclaimer!). In such commitment is possible a depth, wholeness, and peace that we cannot otherwise achieve.

Take, for example, the wisdom of Helen Mayne of Slidell, Louisiana. Helen is a wife, mother, and grandmother. She is also a gifted fabric artist. Blending her love of family and art, she has created her own unique spiritual practice of relationships. After visiting the AIDS quilt in Washington, DC, she wrote this poem, "How to Make an AIDS Quilt":

Prepare a panel the size of a grave
from a heavy cotton the color of love
which is firm enough to support your stitch.

Begin with his name, the name
you gave him the day he was born,
the name above footprints the size of your thumb
that declared him officially yours.

Cut out the letters for appliqué
and pin them down, using color and line
to make a pleasing pattern across the span.

Sew them on firmly, so they cannot work loose,
and make each stitch a memory of part of
his life. Your stitches will have to be small.

Allow your tears to shrink the holes the
needle makes as it draws the thread
to create a permanent meld.

Couch a pet name, and
embroider a phrase he used to repeat
that brings him to life each time you hear it.

Say, at last, how you miss him,
before you finish with
"Love you, Mom."

Helen knows. Commitment is a practice that can continue even long after the one to whom we have committed
has died. Commitment creates an opportunity to practice
awareness, appreciation, and detachment from unimportant
expectations, just like making an AIDS quilt.

Sometimes it is still easy to think of my parenting and
partnering demands as duties that take me away from a more
spiritual time. I still indulge, occasionally, in imagining a
spiritual practice as an activity that requires quiet, calm, and
even isolation. When I slow down and pay attention, though,
another truth becomes clear: The wiping, listening, clean-
ing, hugging, holding, forgiving, helping with homework,
and driving to Little League are all activities within which
we can find connection and renewal, if done with awareness, appreciation, detachment, and commitment. A spiritual practice of everyday relationships is a spiritual practice
that is available to every one of us, wherever and with whom-
ever we live.

Partnership as Spiritual Practice

Brian J. Kiely

Not long ago, I was talking with an older woman friend. For two years she and her husband had lived happily in a small mobile home. They enjoyed each other's company all the time, and there was little friction between them. How did they do it? I asked in amazement. They did it without thinking, she said. It came naturally.

I am not like my friend, or my parents, whose marriage was also long and seemingly easy. I come from an age when one does not necessarily join "for better or worse," never mind for life. I am on my third partnership, and partnership, for me, is far from effortless. I have to work hard to find the elusive equilibrium between me, thee, and us. In fact, for me, partnership has become a spiritual discipline, practiced habitually, intentionally, and with the awareness that the reward is not in the mystical moments of perfect union, but in the journey through the years together.

THE MYSTIC CYCLE AND RELATIONSHIP

The process of becoming a good life partner mirrors the ancient ways of mystical practice outlined by Matthew Fox in his book, *Creation Spirituality*. Fox described mysticism as a round path with four identifiable points in the circle.

The *Via Positiva,* or Positive Way, is life at its most ordinary, with no real problems, hurt feelings, or bruised egos. Time together is relaxed and enjoyable, and conversations are easygoing, lacking the loaded quality they can sometimes take on when phrases like, "What is THAT supposed to mean?" appear as responses to a casual request for clean socks or an unscrambled newspaper. On the other hand, the *Via Positiva* lacks excitement and exhilaration. There are no highs in this stage, no unbridled passion, no exciting new challenges or vistas. Nothing is building in the *Via Positiva* . . . except possibly the inevitable storm clouds of conflict.

The *Via Negativa,* or Negative Way, is the next point on the circle. It is a time when communication is problematic, levels of trust are low, disagreements frequent. To use more religious language, the *Via Negativa* is the walk through hell that is spiritually necessary before rebirth or resurrection. That hell is the creation of both partners in their fear and anxiety about life, in their responses to betrayals of trust or grief for things lost. For some that hell means being too close, noisy battles, even violence. For others, it means the distancing of stony silence and growing apart. While painful, this time spent in the ashes of the relationship is a necessary part of the cycle. Sooner or later we all go through it.

In the *Via Creativa,* or Creative Way, love reasserts itself. It brings a spring-like feeling of renewal as we begin to find our taste for relational life again. We rediscover joy and passion, remember why we fell in love. We recognize that we may, just possibly, have had something to do with our most recent stroll down the *Via Negativa*. We regain the trust that allows us to turn away from face-to-face confrontation in favor of facing the world together. It is here that we encounter our most perfect feelings of love and union. These feelings, however long-lasting or short-lived, keep us in the relationship for the long haul. They keep us coming back for more.

Finally, we achieve the *Via Transformativa,* the Transformational Way. This is the part of the cycle when we build on our insights and make real and lasting change. We work together smoothly as a team; we find imaginative and delightful ways to be with each other. We take no offense at our partner's missteps, and we grow beyond our own self-preoccupation and insularity. It is in this part of the circle that our sense of intimacy deepens, for the trust rebuilt is put into practice and supported by our deeds as much as our words. In the *Via Transformativa*, the relationship truly is transformed, perhaps only in small steps, but in real steps nonetheless.

THE SPIRITUAL PRACTICE

Can we gain something by making partnership a practice that we do intentionally and thoughtfully? I believe we can. The more we can become truly conscious and present to not just our partners, but to our relationships, the more time we can spend in that wonderfully rewarding exhilaration of the *Via Creativa*.

What does it take to make our loving into a spiritual discipline? The things that distinguish all spiritual practices: intentionality, patience, and a willingness to let go of what we want in favor of the gifts we are given. But it all begins with being intentional about being a partner. To reach up for a jar on the top shelf or bend down to tie your shoes is not the same as practicing a careful stretching routine before exercise. In the same way, having the occasional serious conversation with your partner or resolving a fight is not the same as approaching partnership in a disciplined way.

The key to partnering as a spiritual practice is the willingness for both partners to stay involved every day. It is possible to spend years living with another person with relatively little conflict—matched by an equally low level of passion. For some people, that is enough to satisfy their deepest needs. But I have always found too much safety suffocating. I prefer new challenges, new tests. And with my current partner, I am seeking the challenge of depth. Perhaps I have finally learned that a continuing relationship has its own novelty and excitement as over time we unlock new doors of intimacy. It's a bit like the thrill of achieving the next level on a video game instead of giving up and trying a new one. To unlock that next level is a risky business, where the risk is expressed in terms of emotional pain, possibly even the loss of the relationship. But if two people pass through together, the rewards of the next level include understanding, passion, and ever-strengthening ties.

There are four aspects to partnering as spiritual practice: engagement, commitment, individuality, and honesty.

ENGAGEMENT

We live many parts of our lives either by rote or by accident. We can go to work, do the housework, buy the groceries, even raise children without being truly present to those parts of our lives. I frequently meet people who are not really present in their partnerships either. Once, perhaps, they shared long walks and deep talks, but now they eat dinner in front of the television news, communicate only about routine details, and exist as two solitudes *not* meeting and greeting each other. They stop looking into each other's eyes and start looking past the other to the next thing on their agenda.

Choosing to treat partnership as a spiritual practice means bringing your partner's life and feelings and moods back into the active present of your being. It means choosing to be engaged with each other. When we make that choice again and again in a disciplined way, we start the mystical wheel of relationship rolling around. To be engaged is to make your partner a priority in your life, to carve out time together willingly. It is to give up some of the interesting new things life has to offer in order to do the work needed to keep your partnership whole and healthy.

Engagement is not always a safe or simple path. It opens issues and attitudes to shared scrutiny. It means facing our own failings and acts of betrayal. And it means not threatening to end the relationship when things get tough. When we choose to stay engaged with our partners, we give them permission to tell us what they really feel on any issue without the fear of violence or break-up. There is no room for hostage-taking. The price of engagement is the revolving of the mystical wheel, which means occasional visits to the hell of the *Via Negativa*. The reward of engagement is the rebirth and deepening of trust that comes after we pass through that hard time together.

COMMITMENT

Commitment—a daily affirmation of love, made in one's own heart—is the second dimension of the practice. Admittedly, some relationships do not merit a lifelong commitment—those marred by violence or addiction, partnerships that keep each partner from standing alone as an individual, or situations that lack the basic qualities of engagement necessary for this model to work. But a key for allowing a partnership to deepen is a daily decision by both partners that they are committed to making it work in the long term. It is that commitment that allows us to pass through the hard times of the *Via Negativa* with some faith that our partner will walk through with us. Without that faith, without that commitment, the mystic wheel cannot roll. Many relationships never visit the tough issues because one or both partners fear they are not loved enough (or are not worthy of being loved enough) to allow the relationship to survive. And without that faith, the relationship remains superficial.

INDIVIDUALITY

There is still a romantic notion, most often observed in young lovers, that in partnering the two really become one entity. There is an expectation that they will do everything together, share everything, spend each waking moment in each other's company.

I can't think of anything more horrible.

Partnership involves commonality, closeness, and a decision to face life together—but it is not about becoming one.

In *Gift from the Sea,* Anne Morrow Lindbergh likens a good relationship to the dance. The partners know the pattern of the dance and share the rhythm with each other, and yet move within that pattern as individuals. As Kahlil Gibran says in another wedding favorite, "Let there be spaces in your togetherness and let the winds of the heavens dance between you." If partnership is to become a spiritual practice, then the partners have to work continually to affirm the uniqueness of the other. They must take delight in each other's accomplishments outside the partnership, understanding that fulfillment in other aspects of life is no threat to a strong and trusting relationship.

HONESTY

The final aspect of the spiritual practice of partnership is a willingness to be honest with your partner, and, more importantly, with yourself. Many people I know have a great deal of insight about their partner's failings—but in most cases, mine included, we're a little less forthcoming with a catalogue of our own failings and irritating habits.

Marriage manuals have many useful exercises for changing this bad habit, such as active listening or role reversal, but they all require each partner to speak and to listen with honesty. It's often hard to hear the truth, and it sometimes takes a while for us to actually understand it. But if we lack this essential honesty towards the other, or the ability to look honestly at ourselves through our partner's eyes, then the possibility for a long and successful relationship is diminished.

THE PAYOFF

What can we gain by making partnering a spiritual discipline? A blissful existence? Great sex? No more fights? Not necessarily—but what we will gain, as with other spiritual practices, is the realization of wholeness. There will continue to be good and bad times, as well as creative and neutral times. That is the cycle of things. But when we practice partnership as a spiritual discipline, we know there will be good times to go with the bad, and that the relationship will grow in intimacy, care, and love. The partnership grows stronger with each new struggle survived, with each new joy celebrated.

Partnership as spiritual practice has no simple exercises to follow, no ten-minute daily routine. Like every such discipline it takes hard work and the way is often confusing. But if we keep the attitudes of engagement, commitment, individuality, and honesty before us, our rewards will be enriching and deep.

Marriage

M. Maureen Killoran

The alarm rings, and so begins the spiritual discipline that has changed our lives. Neither my husband nor I are morning people, and at our age we tend to sleep poorly, so most days we bring a less than enthusiastic response to the dawn. But still it begins. The alarm rings, and one or the other of us rolls over, switches on the light, and fumbles for a book which is hiding somewhere near the edge of the bed.

Let's say it's my turn to begin. I silently read the page we marked for today and pass the book to my husband who does the same. Then his voice is sleepy, quiet, as he reads aloud . . . . Funny how different the text sounds when I listen . . . . Peter returns the book to me, so that I, in turn, may read aloud to him. For a few minutes, we share our reactions to what we have read, seeking to open our hearts a little wider as we begin the day. Each of us offers a prayer (sometimes we call it a wish) for the coming hours, and then, we close with a simple meditation:

> Grace to us and peace.
> We are given this day,
> and awareness of its colors and sounds;
> these and other gifts, too numerous to name
> and infinitely rare, are given.
> For these gifts,
> we are thankful.

Grace to us, indeed. And peace. I credit this simple morning ritual, coupled with an equally simple one at bedtime, with saving our marriage and changing our lives. To understand this, you need to know where we have been.

Being married did not come easily to Peter and me, although we jumped into it quickly enough some ten years back. Each of us brought middle-aged stubbornness to our union, and neither of us had much experience with compromise or trust. Though we differ in the ways we explain it, the fact is that the first years of our marriage were rough. Our relationship did not come easily, and yet we brought to the union a commitment to the marriage itself, a willed commitment to what we called the "third thing." Transcending our individual egos and self-interest, this commitment held us together even as anger and frustration pushed us apart. And yet there was loneliness and longing for some means of bridging the gulf that was our daily experience of relationship.

It is said that, when we are ready, a teacher will come. A few years ago, I had the good fortune to meet Dr. Vera Mace, who, with her late husband David, pioneered the field of marriage enrichment. To my delight, Vera seemed to enjoy my company as much as I did hers. We spent many afternoons sharing good British tea—and our souls. Vera often spoke of David's and her lifetime commitment to making "better marriages, beginning with our own." At first, her passion evoked in me primarily a sense of regret for the chaos of my own married life. As time went on, however, I began to appreciate the subtleties of this wise nonagenarian's relationship with life—her openness to change, her acceptance of difference, her refusal to give up either on an idea or on prayer. In the empowering warmth of her example, I began for the first time seriously to entertain the possibility that a better marriage might be possible for Peter and me.

And so I had the mentor. I had the desire. My heart was wide open to possibility by the time my friend Linda Bair made me a gift of a modern interpretation of the Rule of St.

Benedict. Benedict was a monk in sixth-century Italy who revolutionized the monastic system of living into a daily rhythm of prayer, work, study, and fellowship. The keys to the Benedictine Rule are intentionality, companionate support, and respect for the irreplaceable details of the mundane. I was reminded of the Zen axiom, "When you are working, work. When you are sitting, sit. Above all, don't wobble."

Although as a couple, my husband and I were skeptical about conventional methods of prayer, the gentle pragmatism of Benedict's ancient Rule appealed to us. Together, we made a commitment to read a brief passage from the Rule every morning. As time went on, we tinkered with this and added that, until our brief reading developed into a ritual, a discipline of the head and the heart that we observe—dare I say religiously?—every day. We prayed—or at least we call it prayer—and out of that prayer has blossomed an astonishing bond of love.

Over time we have drawn on many sources: Benedict, Meister Eckhardt, the *Tao Te Ching,* compilations of poetry, some of the Psalms. Our reflections are usually concrete, focusing on what the passage might mean in the immediate context of our lives. "I've been thinking about all the odds and ends of time I've let go over the years," one of us might say. "All those hours when I believed life was forever. Now I can see the end, feel it coming towards me. No matter what comes along, whether it's good or bad, I don't want to miss a minute of what I have left to live."

Not infrequently we indulge in quiet conversation, sharing ideas or trading intimacies as we let the passage nudge us into a contemplative frame of mind. "I know what you mean. I don't think I've seen more than a couple of dozen sunrises. But I don't want to look backwards. You're right. At our age we can feel the end coming, and I want to be deliberate about looking ahead, appreciating the gifts we have today."

From there, we move into spoken prayer, an expression of intentionality about the day. "Today I will make time for a walk in the middle of the day." "Today I will pay attention to and celebrate the little things around me." "Please, God, help me find the strength for the difficult challenge I have to face this day." "Help me hold in my heart the problems and the suffering of _____, whose life is so very challenging right now."

Then, the ritual prayer, always the same, always said by one of us first and then the other. Although we have drawn on many sources in choosing our daily reading, this prayer of Benedict's we have committed to memory and it is the same for us each day: "Grace to us and peace. . . ."

The day proceeds. We work and celebrate, make mistakes and achieve, laugh and squabble, worry and play. The day proceeds and whether we are better people for having prayed, I cannot tell, but I do know that I at least enter the world more centered, more connected to a relationship that provides an anchor for my values and my life. Prayer has not only saved my marriage; it also has deepened and enriched my life.

We work crazy hours, my husband and I. I'm a minister with lots of night meetings to attend, and he's a maintenance worker on the evening shift. By the time we get home, we are both tired and usually far from our best. For years we fell readily into arguments or, on a good night, into bed, pretty well wrapped up in a book or in ourselves. These days, we're still tired. We still read in bed. But something fundamental has changed. In order to "make better marriages"— at least to improve our own—we spend some time, each night, in what, for us, is prayer.

We begin by taking turns re-reading aloud the passage with which we began our day. Peter reads, or I do, and then the book is passed and we listen to the other, hearing not so much the words as the voice of the beloved. Then—and this is crucial—no matter what kind of mood we are in, we take hands, and give to one another "an appreciation," a gift of words to share something large or little that our partner did that endeared him or her to us today. "When we walked the dog, it made me feel good when you stopped and gave me a kiss. I appreciate that." "I appreciate you for giving me support when I had a hard time giving blood today." And frequently, the words come without bidding: "I love you."

We've discovered that a funny thing happens when you make a habit of ending your day by exchanging appreciations. As we go about our lives, we find ourselves noticing the little things that would otherwise have been ignored. Details become dear—the touch of a hand, a smile in the midst of a tough moment, the lilt of a voice during an otherwise routine exchange. He may not pick up his socks, but we laugh together, sometimes until we cry. I still slide too easily into impatience, but for the first time in my life, "I love you" is an ongoing feeling, not just words I ought to say.

I've come to the conclusion that a daily prayer discipline does not have to be complicated. It does not have to follow a ritual set down by people in a new or an old book. What matters is that you come to the whole business with an attitude of intentionality and with respect for the little things, the gifts of the ordinary that populate your days. What matters is that you find a pattern that fits, and then you stick to it.

And so we do, every day: "Grace to us and peace. . . ." And with these words, with our intentionality, and our hope, has come that for which we hardly dared to pray. My husband and I love each other. Prayer has changed our lives. In our own small way, we, too, are working toward better marriages, beginning with our own. *Deo gratias.*

Parenting

Pat Westwater-Jong

Jess and Alex, your dad and I promise to strive for:

*The patience to listen to you, especially at the most
frustrating times*
*The love to understand and empathize from your per-
spectives*
*The strength to speak the truth to you, to stand up for
what we believe is right and to admit when we are
wrong, and to set good examples for you, to live
our lives as we ask you to live yours*
*The wisdom to respond to you in ways that will help
you to be aware, secure, honest, responsible, compassionate, and loving people—people with self-respect, respect for other people, and for the earth.*

*So let's dance together, let's sing together, let's laugh
and cry together, work and play together! Your dad
and I hope to continue to help you discover, develop,
and delight in the wonderful spirit that shines within
you, Jessica Westwater Jong and you, Alexander Robert Westwater Jong.*

I wrote these words for the Dedication Ceremony for my
two children. It was easier to write than it has been to live,
of course.

The patience to listen to you, especially at the most frustrating times

Occasionally I'm a little short-tempered. Recently I called out to my son, "Will you wash your hands and go practice the piano?" There was an edge to my voice, a sharp edge. I was racing to get chicken in the oven before taking my son to his piano lesson and I couldn't find my apron and I'd just scattered flour all over my sweater. My son was slowly eating a million pomegranate seeds, one by one. There really was no other way to eat it.

I was taking my anger out on him. If a friend my age had been sitting there, I might have cursed my situation, but I wouldn't have used that tone of voice. I never use an impatient tone with my friends. My friends don't dawdle, either. But children do. I sighed and noted my behavior. I apologized for my tone of voice and asked him again in a tone I would like him to use with me. Listening—perhaps the most important key to knowing my spirit and those of my children. First, listening to my children with my ears and eyes and heart. Only by having enough quiet time to really attend to nothing but my own thoughts and those of my loved ones, do I remember to really listen.

Second, listening to my own spirit through meditation helps me hear what my children and I think and feel. Seven years ago, my husband was diagnosed with cancer. During our all-consuming struggle to heal him, I ruptured a disk in my back and started swimming laps to recover. I meditated as I swam. I focused on my breathing always, but I devoted different decades of laps to different subjects.

Many lengths were devoted to my final attempts to heal my husband. By the time I got to twenty lengths, I spent ten thinking about what life might be like for my son. How well do I know him, his special talents and delights, his troubles and blind spots or areas that might need help to develop? How happy does he seem? What are his relationships like? What is our relationship like? I would then spend the next ten lengths or so thinking about life from my daughter's perspective. One night I jumped out of the pool mid-swim to call her from the pool pay phone to apologize for not listening to something she requested on my way out the door. In the first years of swimming after my husband's death, I would sometimes gasp for breath as I cried my way through the water. A couple of times I even stopped briefly at the end of the pool to finish crying so I could breathe enough to swim some more.

Swimming meditation helped me heal my back and my soul. But it was so time consuming, I replaced it with walking meditation through conservation land near my home. For me, meditation is the opposite of daydreaming. If daydreaming is a kind of sleep, meditating is being truly the most awake and conscious I can be. I do three kinds of meditation. The first is like taking my spiritual temperature and helps me to be more disciplined in my thinking and being. I give space for my subconscious to churn and pop up into consciousness whatever is on my mind. As soon as I realize I'm thinking about something, I note it and then let it go. Knowing my problems or joys at that time allows me to let them go, and eventually or periodically, I am at peace.

The second kind of meditation is a focused meditation, time set aside for problem solving, such as reflecting on each child. I consider this a kind of working meditation. I walk my way through my best thinking and sometimes into and through my most painful and angry feelings. My third meditation is pure pleasure. It's where I get my energy. I empty my mind of thoughts, as best I can, and pay attention to nature's beauty and energy. I feel grateful and silently give thanks to the source I can tap to feed me and get me through the day.

The love to understand and empathize from your perspectives

Whether my children volunteer a reaction to what I say, or I have to wonder and ask them for one, or I need to meditate to put myself in their shoes, I must pay attention to what they say and how they seem. If they are feeling pain or anger, for whatever reason, I want to comfort them and try to empathize from their perspective. That doesn't mean I need to agree with them. I need to understand them, and they need to know and feel that they are cared about and understood.

Sometimes I can be generous and give them what they want, sometimes I agree with their perspective. But sometimes what they need is for me to gently and firmly not give them what they are requesting. This could be for their own safety and well-being or a lack of resources or because someone else's needs must come first at that time. I believe that I need to help my children develop values of self-respect and respect for others, learning that happiness does not come from getting everything they think they want, but in learning to accept and appreciate what they have.

The strength to speak the truth to you, to stand up for what we believe is right, and to admit when we are wrong

Sometimes I will decide with hindsight that something I did or said was wrong. My parents didn't feel they had that option. When I was a kid, my dad told me that when he was a boy his parents were always right, he was never allowed to disagree with them. To disagree, no matter how politely, was disrespectful. I can remember as politely as possible making my case for a review of a decision my father had made. He said to me that even if I had a point, he would not go back on his decision because I would not respect him. I remember thinking he was wrong; I would respect him *more* for admitting he was wrong and being able to change his mind. He agrees with me now.

There's been a cultural shift in parent-child relationships. It's a relief to be free to be honest as a parent, but it puts most of us in the challenging position of parent pioneering.

I must balance being open and flexible with being consistent. If I truly listen to my children and am clear about my values, that should help me base my reactions to my children in a way consistent with those values.

To set good examples for you, to live our lives as we ask you to live yours

It can be so hard to know the right thing to do. My parents were stricter than I think was helpful, but I see so many parents giving their children "freedom to be themselves," meaning the freedom to run around without being aware of other people, without learning to be respectful. Sometimes these children yell at or even hit their siblings or their parents without an immediate firm reaction. I don't know any parent who hasn't resorted to yelling on occasion, but I do think using anger to control children's behavior is unnecessary and spiritually unhealthy.

I use time-outs tailored to what I think will best teach each child according to her age, emotional state, the offense, and the lesson that needs to be taught. I started when my children were toddlers. I gently and firmly sat them down in a chair and held them there and counted to three before they could even count themselves. Then I said in a sentence what they should or should not do in the future and an alternative way to ask for what they wanted or for expressing anger. "You don't hurt someone. You don't hit someone. Ask nicely if you want something." As they got older I would send them to their rooms, usually for ten seconds. They can come out after talking with me, as briefly as possible, about their mistake, what to do next time, and offering an apology, if appropriate.

We certainly teach more by example than any other way. I value not hurting people, even if I feel they have hurt me. If I discipline my children by hurting them, my message is it's okay to control others by hurting them. I believe all our spirits are connected, when someone hurts me we both suffer. There is no need to compound this hurt with more hurt. It helps no one. I also believe it is unhealthy to allow a hurtful situation to continue. If someone is hurting me or someone else, it is my responsibility to see if I can do something to stop it. I feel I set limits best when I remember it seems to be normal child behavior to occasionally hurt others and property, and it is my job to teach them not to do this. There is no reason for me to yell or make them feel they are bad. They can feel the pain of hurting someone, take responsibility for it, ask for forgiveness, be forgiven, and put it behind them, all in as few minutes as possible.

To respond to you in ways that will help you to be secure, sensitive, compassionate, and loving people

My children ask what to do on the playground when one child is hurting them or another child. "Stop it, if you can," I say. Can they notice how sad they, and usually others, feel when someone is being hurt? They should try to stop it nonviolently, without doing something wrong themselves. This is not easy. Is there a parent of an elementary school child who hasn't struggled with how to stop fights, whether their child is a victim, an offender, or a bystander? We don't want our children to be bullies, sissies, or tattletales, or people who stand by and allow other people to get hurt. The tools we give them to respond to situations in childhood will be tested and refined into their adult behaviors.

To learn empathy kids must be aware of their own feelings. They must feel their own pain, sadness, and anger, as these will be teaching aids. We don't need to inflict pain on them, or encourage them to inflict pain on themselves; there will be plenty of pain in their lives. Pain, repressed or not healed, may motivate a child to lash out and hurt someone else. That repressed pain and retaliating hurtful behavior is spritually damaging to everyone involved. Instead, we can help them use their pain to learn compassion. We can say, "remember how sad you felt when 'x' or how angry you felt when 'y'?" and they will have an emotional memory to log back to as a frame of reference for that feeling—they will understand how others feel. If we comfort them through their disappointments, they learn how to comfort others. They can learn that it feels better to empathize and comfort someone than it does to hurt someone. And if the person isn't ready to be comforted, well, kids have probably felt that also, and can learn to sense when someone just needs to be left alone.

To be people with self-respect, respect for other people, and for the earth

I believe I need to let my children know and graciously accept that they are each precious individuals, with their own special strengths and gifts, just as every other person on earth is. They are more important in my heart than any other children. And each of them is as important as any other person on earth regardless of intelligence, talent, physical beauty, age, sex, job, race, wealth, country or religion. But each of them is no more important than any other person, regardless of intelligence, talent, physical beauty, job, age, sex, race, wealth, country or religion. And if we happen to belong to a race, class, or country that has more power or dominance than another, it is our responsibility to respect and pay special attention to those with less power, to share our power, and to listen to and assist those with less voice.

I cherish my time outside enjoying nature's beauty. I feel my spiritual health is in part dependent upon the health of our planet. My kids have shared my lifestyle and also love the woods and mountains and oceans that are so important to me. I must admit, I bribed them occasionally when they were really young. Initially, I think they found coming inside for cocoa as much fun as sledding and building snowmen. But we started wintertime fun together in small doses and I didn't force them to stay ouside longer than they were comfortable. They have grown to enjoy the earth's gifts in all seasons. I've taken the kids camping. They are proud of their fire-building skills and have been awed by stars in a black sky reflected in a black lake. I share literature from environmental organizations to teach us all ways in which our earth is in peril. We work together to recycle and try to buy foods and household and garden products that aren't poisonous. We do not live an environmentally pure lifestyle, but we do enjoy the earth, inform ourselves of perils, and take responsibility to contribute to the environmental health of the earth.

So, let's dance together, let's sing together, let's laugh and cry together, work and play together

This is the fun part. But that doesn't mean it's always easy. Our lives can get so fast that rushing from one commitment to the next takes so much time we don't leave enough time for having fun. It doesn't have to cost any money, just time.

I think each child needs a way to express him- or herself, the inner self, artistically. In my family we all enjoy music. I remember my mother playing Wagner's *Die Walkure* on the record player for my siblings and me while we all galloped around the house like horses. How many women remember their dads teaching them to dance while standing on their dad's feet? I've taught my kids to waltz while my son sits on my daughter's shoulders so the three of us can dance together. Before a recent piano recital my son was trying to prepare his favorite song by playing it as fast as he could. I said it didn't matter how fast he played, I loved hearing it most when he played it from his heart, when he played it as though he loved every note. He now plays it with a passion that expresses his spirit—when he's angry he pounds it and when he's happy, the notes ring with joy.

One of the questions I ask myself when I walk is have we laughed, danced, sung, volunteered to the community together recently? We walk in the woods together. We gather trash and recycle together. We work in the garden together, sometimes we treat ourselves to ice cream or a bike ride or a story after our work. I have told my children that I believe each day we're alive is a gift. In exchange for this gift we need to give back a little something each day. They agree.

Your dad and I hope to continue to help you discover, develop, and delight in the wonderful spirit that shines within you

My father is very ill, possibly dying. My children and I talk about this together. I started to cry in the car the other day and told my son I was sad because my dad might die soon. I asked him if he was sad, too. He looked like he might cry and nodded. I put my hand on his arm and nodded back. We have cried together through his dad's death. I can't expect them to feel sad at the same times and in the same ways I do. I'm a private person, but I feel it's important I express my sadness and invite them to express theirs. So I'm as honest and open as I can be about my feelings, all of them, and ask them about theirs. I'm learning as we go through these times how each child likes to express his or her grief.

I share with them my beliefs about death and ask them what they think. I tell them that I believe God is a spirit, an energy, perhaps love, that is the essence of my soul. When Jess was five she announced "When you die, you die and *that is it.*" Now that she's ten, she says she's not so sure. I ask, share, listen, discuss what feels true to them and me, and I have found their spirits to be as wise as mine. This is my job as a parent, to help discover, develop, and delight in these wonderful spirits that shine within my children.

Each night, right after I turn off my daughter's light, she likes a back rub with heavy pressure. I marvel at this ten-year-old, so old and young, depending on the minute. Sometimes, as I rub my son's back, I ask him how his day was, did anything make him happy or sad that day? He's not much of a talker on his own, so usually he likes me to ask him a question.

Last night he said he wished he could turn back time so he could start his back rub over and over and it would never end. Sometimes I am tired myself, or in a hurry to get to a meeting, or thinking about getting to folding the laundry or washing the dishes or—stop! The spiritual value for me and for my child is being all the way with him at that moment, noticing what his back is like at age eight, that his head is shaped like his dad's, that he's sad about ripping his favorite pants that day, which if I am fully listening with my heart and hands, is so endearing it allows my love for him to rise and sometimes move me to tears.

What can be more exquisite than one's child ending his day and opening to sleep, laughing about something silly or struggling with the injustice of a boy who cheats in a game during recess? This is truly listening—and when I tune in this way, my heart opens to these little people entrusted to my care, and our spirits meet in love.

Loss and Grief

Jennie Knoop

Loss is a tearing of the soul, and so the work of grieving is a work of healing and growth. There can be unbelievable pain, especially when what is lost is part of your being. When my oldest daughter Ericka was murdered in April 1993, it felt to me that the fabric of the universe itself was torn. As I descended, sometimes by tiny steps, sometimes tumbling down headlong into the process of mourning her, I found that I was opening to a force almost dismembering in its intensity. I began a journey of healing that is still in process and will always touch me in some way. Nearly four years later I am opening packages in my heart that contain glimpses of her agony, glimpses I couldn't have handled before.

We wisely protect ourselves from fully experiencing shock, loss, and trauma. We can wall off and freeze what would shatter us beyond recovery. But this exacts a physical and spiritual price that increases over time. The internal pressures of unresolved pain can spur us to seek numbness in ultimately self-destructive addictions. Physical pain or illness is another common by-product of this repressive coping. While I respect the age-old wisdom that time heals all wounds, I've found it safer, easier, and less painful to consciously engage in the pursuit of healing day by day.

Crying is the greatest of all spiritual practices for releasing grief and healing from loss. Still, even those of us who sniffle at sentimental commercials may have problems opening to the devastation of tears that feel like they will go on forever. Unfortunately, those are the very tears we need to shed. It's easy to get caught in a pattern of resisting them until they break through in an overwhelming, painful bout of crying, after which we are even more resistant to opening to grief. Choosing to spend a few minutes a day doing practices to support grieving can make a big difference. Instead of draining contraction and ongoing pain and depression, there can be a sense of release, of refreshment and luminous peace after your tears.

I'm very good at derailing my grieving by shifting unconsciously to a mental process of observing, trying to understand what the tears are about or what triggered them. This thinking tends to shut down the emotional flow quickly. While this way of maintaining control may have been desirable when my grief was too great to be contained, it has been counterproductive in the long run. I discovered that my busy brain, trying so hard to keep the pain at bay, could be invited into unity with my emotions if I held the thought "I feel sad." Then, my tears would begin to flow without obstruction or resistance.

You can easily create your own mantra to help yourself open more fully into the release of sorrow, or anger, or whatever emotions are presenting as part of your healing work. The words "I feel," spoken inwardly to yourself, can acknowledge your struggle and create a unity from which release can flow. For body-wide, diffuse feelings of grief, depression, or emotions that won't quite come to the surface—that heavy feeling—I've found lying down and holding an image or memory that evokes strong feelings works well to enable release.

When grieving, many people seek refuge in blame. But I am convinced that blaming is only an attempt to retain a sense of control. I watched all of us—the members of my family, the family of the young man who had killed Ericka, and then himself—struggle to assign the blame for their deaths, to explain how such an unbearable tragedy could occur. It is true that human malice and error cause many deaths. But if you are grieving, your loss will still be there when you've figured out exactly who did what wrong. For your sake, please try to bypass blame. And please don't torture yourself with if-only thoughts. Spot these efforts to regain a sense of control for what they are. If you can bypass blame of self and others, you can dampen the oscillation and sharp edges of brokenness that often continue to wound and prolong the tragedy, and move instead towards healing.

It can be liberating to actively seek the process of healing, to know that you are working to make it happen. Years ago when I was a Lamaze teacher of techniques for labor and birth, we used the image of waves to describe the intense muscle contractions of labor. As swimmers know, the water will support you if you relax and flow with it. A sailor will tell you to head right into the waves in rough weather. For mothers giving birth and people who are grieving, relaxation and openness, good support, and mastery of simple skills can make the difference between drowning in pain and a calm voyage. Tension and resistance work far less well.

I want to share a breathing practice that has been in use for over three thousand years that came to me through the lineage of the great Sufi, Hazrat Inayat Khan. It is a practice that supports clearing and release and deepens a nourishing, healing connection to the cosmos. It is a simple yet powerful tool that has enabled many people in many kinds of pain to help themselves. For myself, this practice has been a source of deep healing, opening the doors and windows that pain closes, again and again.

ELEMENTAL PURIFICATION BREATH

This practice is a series of four different breaths, done slowly five times each. Stand gently, feet slightly apart with soft knees, facing a window. It's OK to do this practice in bed when you're ill or on cold mornings, and outdoors is wonderful.

1. Earth Breath—Breathe in through the nose, then out through the nose, five times. *Relax your feet, legs, and pelvic floor. Drop your bottom. On the inhale feel the nurturing energy of the earth rise, surrounding and renewing you. On the exhale, visualize the magnetism of the earth below you drawing and clearing toxins, pain, whatever needs releasing.*

2. Water Breath—In nose, out mouth, five times. *Relax your reproductive organs and lower abdomen. Visualize standing in a shower or waterfall that is cleansing and refreshing. Draw that waterfall through the crown of your head on the inhale, diffusing it through your body on the exhale, rinsing away impurities and fatigue. Feel all that is dry being moistened and transfused.*

3. Fire Breath—In mouth, out nose, five times. *Open your solar plexus and heart and suck the breath strongly into this area. Visualize your breath like a bellows feeding an inner fire, melting and burning dross and waste, whatever needs transforming. On the exhale, visualize the breath moving out through the heart, carrying the ash and smoke with it. In addition to the exhale through the heart, you can also visualize the breath leaving through the crown of your head.*

4. Air Breath—In and out mouth, five times. *This is a very shallow, subtle breath. Feel your mouth surrendered and relaxed, barely open. Visualize winds gently caressing your neck. With the slightest draw, let the breath move into and out of your throat, maintaining the sense of the breath's connection to the vastness of air, sky, and space. Enjoy the spaces between the breaths as pure stillness, pure freedom.*

As you finish, offer a prayer or hold a healing intention in your heart. After a week or so of daily practice, you'll find yourself entering quickly into relaxation. The breath work softens pain, anxiety, and resistance like natural anesthesia, enabling you to work within. You might begin to cry or feel other emotions arising as you do this practice. You may feel your body unwinding—wanting to stretch or move into a different posture. By all means, surrender to what is coming up, using your I-feel statement to support the flow if necessary. Do the practice as often as you need to. Every morning will provide a support that sometimes can be felt all day long.

Here's another practice for those of you who, like myself, deal with grief by staying busy and keeping moving. After Ericka was killed, I bought a clear quartz crystal heart and a tiny silk bag to house it. I carried it in my pocket whenever possible. It called to my fingers as I sat in meetings, or listened to another in pain, or watched TV with my other children, Liz and Theo. It went on altars, on dresser tops in motel rooms, and stayed by my bed at night, a gentle reminder of beauty, love, and loss. This soothed and comforted me the way a favorite blanket works to calm a small child. It was a concrete reflection of the grief process within, allowing me to hold my bereavement and my beloved daughter as I moved through the roles my life demanded of me. Recently I cleansed the heart with cool running water and gave it to Ericka's sister, Liz, to help her in her own healing and grieving.

If you've been avoiding a confrontation with your grief or have been unable to touch it, you may find yourself dealing at first with a stockpile of pain and resistance. If so, you can prepare for a rough entry by arranging for bodywork, group, or counseling support. In many communities, hospices offer free bereavement support groups. Be brave, get help, and trust the power you have to effectively grieve and heal. My two greatest problems have been the terrifically unavoidable nature of the pain, and the fear that there was something wrong with me, that it would never get any better. What I've learned is that vast resources within us and around us are unceasingly working for healing.

Starfish can generate new limbs. What we do is better, because what is generated by our growth and healing is far more than what we were before—a weaving of love from our pain, creativity, and the riches of our souls.

ENGAGING THE WILL

Right Action

Spiritual Practice for Our Time

Rebecca Parker

Not long ago, I was at my family's home on Puget Sound. I woke up early and sat with a cup of coffee to watch the dawn light rise over the tall cedars and slant down through the mist that was hovering over the still water. How beautiful the world is, I thought to myself. What a blessing to be alive.

It isn't always so. In his essay "The Fire Next Time," James Baldwin narrates the depth of loss and grief experienced by people of African descent in North America. He shows how self-loathing grows in a culture that tells a child his presence is not welcome, how a sense of the sacredness of other human beings is lost, how ugliness comes into all aspects of living, and how despair descends over people's lives.

Yet, at the end of the essay, Baldwin invokes the rhythms of jazz, the resilience of people hard oppressed, and the freshness of new life he sees in children. The question remains, he says, "What to do with all this beauty?"

This question challenges me more than any other in life. How do I live in a way that keeps faith with beauty—with the beauty I have known, the beauty of all people everywhere, the beauty of the earth? How do I resist the violence that tears us from one another and the earth? When the violence goes deep into the core of the human soul, as it has mine, how is the heart restored?

As I have struggled with these questions, I have come to understand that if I am to recover from violence, live in love, and contribute to healing and transformation, I need to engage in spiritual practices that preserve knowledge beyond what the dominant culture tells me about who I am.

We live in a dominating culture that has been variously named mechanistic materialism, mind/body dualism, white supremacy, or patriarchy. It finds its embodiment in an increasingly globalized economic system that defines human beings as self-interested individuals with an insatiable need for goods. Its economic theories ignore the value of the earth's resources, and it is historically rooted in a construction of hierarchies that justifies the exploitation of people of color. It dulls our capacity to feel and alienates us from the knowledge of our intimate connectedness with one another and the earth.

The spiritual numbness of the dominating culture is at the heart of its violence. Overt acts of violence against one another and against the earth emerge from a more covert violence: the loss of our capacities to feel and think. This loss happens through the suppression of the senses, of desire and of feeling; through the exile of pain and grief; and through the silencing of human dependence on one another and the earth. Critical analysis alone will not disempower this culture, nor will it change its effects. We need to recover our abilities to think and feel. Anesthetization needs to end in our lives.

I find two spiritual practices especially helpful as pathways to doing this. These practices are simple and ancient, but they ask a great deal of those who follow them. I recommend them to you.

The first religious practice is keeping the Sabbath. To keep the Sabbath means, once every seven days, to step outside the dominating culture and enter another space. On a regular basis, stop participating in life as it is defined for us. Choose one day out of seven to not go shopping. To not do any work. To not bring any work home. Instead, give yourself and your family the space to feel what it is hard to feel when you spend all your time, as the poet says, "getting and spending and laying waste your powers." Give yourself time to notice. Walk in the woods and see how the leaves of the willows are coming out, the azaleas are budding, there is a sweetness in the air and the tulips are bending in the wind. Give yourself time to sit at the table with friends, to welcome the friendless into your home, to talk with one another. Give yourself time to read, think, and reflect. Gather with a religious community to pray and give thanks. Open yourself to the wisdom of religious tradition, rituals of reconciliation and hope, liturgies of joy, acts of remembrance and sorrow. Stop the madness and rest. Open yourself to the beauty and the meaning of life, to all those tender capacities in yourself and all those dear relationships with others that are to be cherished. Find a way to know the things that the marketplace can neither give nor take away.

Also in this Sabbath space, give yourself the room to feel the sadness that comes with facing the fact that life on our planet is at risk and that the many forms of violence fracture the bonds of communion and break the heart. Attend to your own despair. Allow yourself to grieve and to nourish the wellspring of our own faithfulness and courage. We cannot offer the world the religious leadership it needs unless we cultivate in ourselves a deep and sustained knowledge of the beauty of life, the reality of sorrow, the goodness of one another, the richness of the world's religious wisdom, and the providence of life's bounty. This is asked of us now.

My own practice of Sabbath keeping is imperfect, but I persist. On Sundays I go to church and take time to be with people I love. I savor life, reflect and feel. I try not to do chores or work but to hold still in the presence of life's tragedy and beauty.

To keep the Sabbath is a radical act of resistance to a culture that has lost track of the meaning of life. From this place of Sabbath keeping, I become more capable of entering into sustained engagement with the culture of which we are all part and which needs our active creative witness and our work for change.

The second spiritual practice that I find helpful is just as simple, just as ancient, and perhaps even more unfamiliar. This spiritual practice is tithing. To tithe is to give ten percent of your income for the common good.

When I comment tithing to you, I am not suggesting tithing in spirit, tithing in principle, or tithing as metaphor. I am suggesting giving away ten percent of your income. It can be difficult, but it can be learned. In fact, I don't think that anyone who tithes has come to it by anything other than learning it. If you've never done it, start with one percent, then move to two, then to three. Work your way to ten percent, step by step. You don't have to give it all to one place. You can give part of it to your church and part of it to people and places that work for the healing and transformation of life.

I count myself lucky to have been taught to tithe as a child and to have learned to incorporate it as a regular practice in my life. In the third grade, when my parents gave me my first allowance of fifty cents, they told me what ten percent of fifty cents was. They gave me a pledge card to the church and a box of offering envelopes. My first tithe was five cents a week to the church.

I have come to believe tithing is so worth doing not just because there are good causes that will flourish if I am able to share my resources, though there are and I believe it is important to do so. Nor it is simply because the tithing of many conservatives has allowed the religious right to gain influence, and I want to support an alternative vision of the good society. There is a deeper, more fundamental spiritual reason why I tithe. I became aware of it when listening to a member of the first congregation I served. It was pledge drive Sunday. People had been asked to talk about why they give to church. Steve De Groot talked about why he tithed.

"I first began to tithe," he said, "because I was taught to obey the teachings of my church, and tithing was one of them. I tithed because I saw obedience as the heart of faithfulness. When I began to understand that obedience was not all that important and could be evil, I continued to tithe because a different reason had come to me. The people I loved most and admired tithed: my parents and leaders in our church. Their lives challenged me by their goodness. I wanted to be like them so I tithed to model my life on theirs."

Steve went on. "But then, I matured in my faith: I came to my own reason for tithing. This is why I do it now: I tithe because it tells the truth about who I am. If I did not tithe, it would say that I was a person who had nothing to give, or I was a person who received nothing from life, or I was a person who did not matter to the larger society, or I was a person whose life's meaning was solely in providing for my own needs. But in fact who I am is the opposite of all those things. I am a person who has something to give. I am a person who has received abundantly from life. I am a person whose presence matters in the world. I am a person whose life has meaning because I am connected to and care about many things larger than myself alone. If I did not tithe, I would lose track of these truths about who I am. By tithing, I remember who I am."

This is the endangered knowledge in our culture that can be preserved by religious practices that teach us a different sense of who we are.

Like all of us, I know I am at risk of forgetting or never coming to deeply know that to be a human being is to live in a world that provides richly for human life, including mine, a world that is to be stewarded, not abused. I do not want to lose track of this knowledge. We are in a world that has enough land to feed all of earth's people and that has enough resources to shelter all of earth's children. If I forget this, and if I forget that my presence matters, then I fail to act as a person who blesses life and who contributes to *tikkun o'lam*— mending the world. I become, instead, complicit with violence, a numbed and alienated soul, who has surrendered to untruth.

By tithing and keeping the Sabbath, I open myself up to what the old theologians called the means of grace. I keep myself open to remembering who I am and what life is, what is precious and what it is to feel, what it is to be connected intimately to earth, to history, to other human beings and what it is to live justly. When I remember this, I know what to do with all the beauty.

I know, with Rumi, "There are a thousand ways to kneel and kiss the ground."

Social Justice

Art McDonald, Deborah Holder, and Stephen H. Furrer

Some people associate the word *spirituality* with a certain sort of person, someone quiet, pious, even austere. But for many, ourselves included, the meaning of words like *religious* or *spiritual* was altered by the Civil Rights and anti-war movements in the 1960s and 1970s. The Reverend Dr. Martin Luther King, Jr., and his allies changed what it meant to be a religious person. The radical liturgical and spiritual practices of the Christian anti-war activists Dorothy Day, Daniel Berrigan, and Phillip Berrigan also brought a change in our thinking. We were captivated by their practice of raiding and attempting to destroy draft files in order to disrupt the draft. Their anti-war, anti-nuclear efforts were something new—skillful acts of civil disobedience, but also far more. They were a spiritual practice.

These activists prayed before, during, and after each action. We were amazed—and deeply moved—by the sight of these women and men kneeling in prayer in front of nuclear missiles only to be handcuffed and incarcerated. Liturgies, we learned, often preceded their actions. To make the idea of sacrifice real, these spiritual warriors frequently poured their own blood on draft files.

This new coming together of prayer, reflection, and activism brought many of us a completely new understanding of spirituality and spiritual practice. Suddenly spiritual practice was embodied. No longer about flight from the world, it was immersion in the world—immersion that aimed to enlist all of our spiritual power in the service of social, cultural, and political transformation.

The African and African-American religious tradition seems to exemplify this embodied spirituality. A friend of ours, an African-American community activist, relates what happened one evening when she spoke about her work. An elderly black church member approached her afterward. "Gail," the woman said, "it was so wonderful to hear you this evening. You are such a spiritual person!" Dumbfounded, Gail said later that she had no idea what the woman meant. "How can I be spiritual?" she exclaimed. "I'm an atheist!" This elderly listener was expressing the notion that justice-making and spiritual wholeness go hand-in-hand, two sides of the same coin. What begins as mysticism ends in social action.

This understanding of spiritual practice as engagement in the world, not withdrawal from it, has been deepened by our sisters and brothers in Asia, Latin America, and Africa. These liberation theologians and practitioners who have experienced sexism, racism, and classism have developed a spirituality that helps to overcome their oppressions—growing within, by working to alleviate suffering out there.

The African (Ghana) feminist theologian Mercy Amba Oduyoye confirms this holistic understanding when she defines spirituality as simply "the energy by which one lives and which links one's worldview to one's style of life." This is a simple, direct explanation of the spiritual life, yet one that speaks directly to the oneness at the center of our being. Paraphrasing the Salvadoran liberation theologian Jon Sobrino, we must deepen our notion of what it means to practice "political holiness."

Recognizing the systemic dimensions of oppression in modern life, one's religious life must begin in solidarity with the oppressed and must result in community. In the words of the slain Archbishop of El Salvador, Oscar Romero, "Religion held with deep conviction leads to political involvement."

What does such a spiritual practice look like in today's United States of America? The model that we use has grown out of the experience many of us had as part of the base community movement in Latin America. Such communities come together and employ an action/reflection model of interaction, in which experiences of oppression are shared, analyzed, and prayed about in light of the community's faith and values. The group's community activism is guided—and often redirected or changed—to truly reflect what it is trying to accomplish. The model serves as a kind of circle in which experience and action, analysis and reflection, prayer and sharing of faith all flow in and out of one another as one practice.

Spiritual practice in Latin American base communities mobilizes one's energy—and links it to others—toward the goal of harmonizing lifestyle with worldview. Adapting the base community model to a North American context has led us to involvement in a local interfaith group operating a multifaceted social service/advocacy agency that provides shelter for homeless men, a food pantry for local families and individuals, and a program of transitional housing for those trying to escape homelessness. We also do considerable advocacy around issues of hunger, homelessness, welfare reform, and economic injustice.

As always with the action-reflection model, we could argue endlessly about which should come first: the analysis or the active experience itself. But for the sake of argument, let's say we came to the decision intuitively that in our community context the issues of hunger and homelessness were the ones to focus on first. This decided, we started to act. First we signed up to cook and serve meals to the men in the homeless shelter. This, we thought (and still believe), is a critical first step toward creating what the black American theologian Thandeka has called "sacred encounters" with other human beings. We quickly discovered that cooking and serving at the shelter was not enough. If the encounter is to be an encounter—one that approaches the sacred—we must do what we can to bridge the distance between our service and the residents by talking and eating with them.

Thus, we also began to engage in other aspects of the social justice cycle by organizing lobbying efforts within local congregations—for instance, letter writing and congressional visiting around welfare, food stamps, and related issues. We encourage ministers to preach on these issues, and we do what we can to organize religious education programs about homelessness and hunger. We join with other local advocacy groups to stage periodic marches to raise consciousness about hunger and homelessness, and we try to put the pressure on politicians. We work with local activists such as the Religious Task Force on the Economy, who are initiating a Living Wage Campaign to force the city government to pay decent wages, and the Alliance for Progressive Action, who have led the fight to maintain quality public broadcasting.

Activities like these form the basis of our spiritual practice. They flow from our faith, our values, our reflection and analysis, and our prayers. We also know that it's important to come together and think about the actions we have taken. As part of that process we read and analyze in an attempt to understand why there is such need. Our reflection and analysis involve sharing our action experiences and exploring the roots of the problems we're seeking to overcome. Why is there an ever-widening gap between our country's (and the world's) haves and have-nots? Why are food pantries and shelters under continually increasing pressure to provide more space and services? We want to understand just what is happening in our society, because we want our actions to be effective.

We also believe that, in order to be effective, our actions must ultimately address the root causes of injustice. We are not just about service but also change. And we are not just about societal, institutional change but also about personal change, the psychological and spiritual change that comes when you live and work in a community committed to justice-making. We believe we must each be willing to be held accountable to one another and to the principles we hold sacred. So we practice supporting and challenging one another to become more human, able to face the consequences of compassionate communal accountability. Today, at the end of the twentieth century, any collective action is not only revolutionary but also a much-needed antidote to a dominant commercialized and hypermobile monoculture that increasingly celebrates manic individualism and overconsumption. In such a world, our communal action and reflection become a healing corrective and provide a powerful model of a justice-seeking community of resistance.

Learning about and practicing anti-oppressive behaviors while celebrating the Spirit means moving beyond unexamined and insight-limiting assumptions into more inclusive communities of trust and support. Reflection on both our tasks and the process of achieving those tasks provides us with opportunities for sacred encounters. This kind of work not only thwarts feelings of powerlessness and alienation, but even more important, it puts us in direct relationship with the mystery at the center of our faith, where justice is forever newly revealed. This work provides us with shared and confirming experiences of grace—a tangible, commonly experienced grace that regularly discloses to us our collective identity as a part of something far bigger than ourselves. In supporting one another through both the successes and the failures of this struggle and helping one another become more compassionate and fully human, we begin to recognize and feel our true identity in God.

Finally, in our activist communities, we share our values and our beliefs. We seek to make our actions consistent with what we say we believe. We pray and meditate from our different religious perspectives to remain connected to the center and core of our beings. Sometimes in our prayers and meditations we sing or use words, sometimes we are silent. Sometimes we use candles or other images that help us remain focused on our task. One of us finds a painting of rifle-toting Harriet Tubman leading slaves to freedom on the underground railroad. Another shares stories handed down by an Appalachian grandmother. In many ways, this spiritual practice takes some important cues from our Latin American, African, and Asian sisters and brothers. Following their example, we believe that any spirituality must begin with a sense of deep solidarity with the oppressed. We reject any spirituality that involves transcending the suffering of our dispossessed brothers and sisters across the globe. We believe that a sense of oneness with their struggle is the ground for all spiritual practice.

Jon Sobrino reminds us that "without historical, real life there can be no such thing as spiritual life." This doesn't mean that spiritual practice is only about activism. Though we believe justice is at the center of authentic spirituality, its realization requires a deep need to be quiet. Meditative practice is critical. Still, we believe that religion without social action is idolatry. We must be clear about the truth of the real, a world full of injustice and inequality.

A living spiritual practice is not always easy. Activists are often tempted to overextend themselves, to fill days and nights with constant action. Such behavior is understandable given the depths of the injustices that exist. But whenever we act in such a manner, our activity becomes less than a spiritual practice and more a one-dimensional attempt to deny the spiritual roots of religious activism.

Many of us find it difficult to remain faithful to our spiritual practice, either because we are not always effective or successful, and we simply tire out, or we face opposition and find it too painful to carry on. That is, living out such a prophetic spirituality often means running into real opposition and rejection from those who disagree or are themselves part of the problem. Keeping in mind that God didn't call us to be successful but to be faithful, we strive to remain faithful so that we may grow spiritually. The difficulties inherent in such a spiritual practice mean that we will often be tempted to abandon it. Perseverance becomes a key part of our practice.

There is good news in all this. Social justice as spiritual practice means that we are about the task of healing and rebuilding the community. It means we are trying to overcome solipsistic and spiritually inauthentic withdrawal. Remaining faithful to such a practice also means reconnecting with the whole, whether one calls that whole God, the beloved community, or the other. Ultimately, this is a hopeful spiritual practice, filled with huge imagination and energy.

If we as religious people and as guardians of religious institutions don't center our spiritual practice in justice-making, then the pain and brokenness fostered by our escalating social divisions will perpetuate, furthering the need to develop inauthentic spiritualities based on withdrawal and separation. After all, we do have the option to build higher fences, lock more doors and construct more prisons. The choice is ours. We believe that social justice as a spiritual practice is an option against such a future, a way to build a more just and loving world. At their heart, all religious traditions are based on this notion of spirituality.

Social justice may seem like a spiritual practice only for the few or strong-hearted. For anyone who read the book or saw the film *Dead Man Walking,* a true story about a New Orleans nun who became a chaplain to prisoners on death row, it is clear that Sister Helen Prejean had no idea what she was in for when she agreed to start writing to a condemned inmate. Her realization of the injustice of the death penalty set her on a journey to bring an end to capital punishment. Her spiritual life became centered around a whole new practice. Today, all of her energies are devoted to this effort. Following the path of social justice, she discovered her whole self.

Such a notion of spiritual practice is ultimately about relationship—with one another and with the whole. It is a spiritual practice about sacred encounters. By grappling with injustice and inequality as a starting point, we go beyond our own experience and into the world of others. Such a practice begins by being honest about social and political inequity and by calling together other people of faith who seek to build a better world. With the realization that action and reflection are really two complementary aspects of one, unified existence, social justice as spiritual path becomes a natural rhythm of the life of faith.

Anti-Racism

Dorothy May Emerson

As a white person, I have the privilege of choosing whether or not to notice racism, whether or not to deal with the racist system in which I live. As a person of faith and conscience who is committed to the struggle to end racism, however, I choose to notice racism. I choose to act in ways that interrupt and challenge the racist structures that surround me. Naturally, noticing and challenging racism are much easier said than done. That is why anti-racism has become for me a central focus of my spiritual practice.

Some years ago I began a spiritual journey to understand and challenge racism within myself and in the systems in which I participate. As with many spiritual journeys, mine began with what others have called a "dark night of the soul." One summer I worked for an organization that mobilized women to promote peace and justice. The African-American woman with whom I shared my position quit—because of the organization's racism and because of mine. She didn't explain her decision in depth; she was tired of having to teach white women about racism, and she told me that I needed to figure out what it meant to live in a racist society for myself. Now, I know that she was right. But at the time, I was devastated. I simply did not understand how my own perception of myself as a completely unprejudiced person who stood up for all people's rights could be so wrong. This was much more than cognitive dissonance. It was a complete denial of something very basic to my sense of who I was.

What happened that summer gave me food for thought and emotions to process for many years to come. I realized that I would never be whole, I would never be who I thought I was and who I wanted to be, unless I could understand how my actions and attitudes were racist. I knew I did not want to be racist, but I realized that I did not know what it would mean not to be racist.

That spiritual journey has taken me through many twists and turns. I came to understand so much that summer—about how racism is built into "the way things are supposed to be," about how I had missed opportunities for questioning and transformation, about how ignorance and idealism caused me to make unwarranted assumptions and blinded me to problems that did exist. Over the years that followed, I encountered others who confronted me about my racism. It was painful beyond description. At times I wanted to retreat from the commitment to anti-racism I had made, and, as a white person, I knew I had the luxury of turning away from this work. But it would not leave me alone for very long. Something would always happen to remind me that I would never be whole until I learned what it meant to be anti-racist.

What I now understand to have been one of the major stumbling blocks for my organization in dealing with racism continues today in many of the groups in which I participate. There is a general failure to understand and address racism on institutional and systemic levels. As long as we persist in thinking of racism as personal prejudice, I do not believe we will be capable of creating the world of justice and peace that we seek. This is why I have chosen anti-racism as a spiritual practice.

Describing the spiritual practice of anti-racism, as I understand and am learning to practice it, is relatively simple, though doing it on a daily basis is not. I approach this practice with techniques and insight gained from Buddhist Insight Meditation (Vipassna). This form of meditation involves quieting your mind by carefully observing your breath as it goes in and out of your nostrils, as your chest rises and falls, or as your abdomen goes in and out. The first part of the practice of anti-racism likewise involves paying attention, only instead of watching your breath, you watch the world around you and within you. And you watch using a particular lens, the lens of race.

Paying attention in this way is something that comes quite naturally to most African Americans and to many other people of color in this culture. For them, it is a matter of survival. They learn early on what to expect from white society, how to act so the chances are greater they will be safe, how to steel themselves against the inevitable snubs, their own fear and that of others, and minor and major acts of aggression. What I am learning to do is to observe these same things, both as they happen to people of color around me and as they don't happen to me. At an anti-racism meeting one day, I became aware that this practice of paying attention had affected my perspective when one of the white leaders commented that, most of the time, he simply was not aware of white privilege, of the benefits he received on a daily basis from being white. I knew that, in time, if he was committed to doing the work of anti-racism, he would become more observant.

After this incident, I became more intentional about paying attention both to the daily benefits I receive as a white person and to the occurrence of acts of racism around me. I also pay careful attention to my own responses both to the acts themselves and to people of color I encounter in my life. Additionally, I watch the media for discussions and dialog about race and racism, and I pay particular attention when this topic emerges in various arenas of public discourse I encounter. By paying attention to race and racism, to the subtle and not-so-subtle ways racism is embedded in virtually every aspect of our lives, I believe I am taking an important step outside my proscribed role as a white person in this society. This is what I would call part one of the spiritual practice of anti-racism.

Naturally, one cannot make such observations without wanting to do something about the situation. Part two of this practice is education. Although I would certainly encourage you to do whatever you can to challenge blatant acts of racism you might encounter, the insidious nature of racism today is that it is subtly and intrinsically woven into the very fabric of our social systems. It needs to be understood as an institutional and systemic problem. Dismantling racism, therefore, requires thoughtful study and analysis. Much of this education can be accomplished through reading books and other literature and viewing movies and videos. There is a vast course of study available, and new resources are being developed constantly, as more and more people take up this spiritual practice.

In addition to your personal study, I would strongly recommend that you find a group of people to work with. By paying attention to discussions of race in your organization or local community, you will undoubtedly discover others who are similarly concerned. And, I would strongly recommend that you participate in some sort of anti-racism training.

Here I need to make an important distinction. Look for the word "anti-racism" rather than "diversity" in descriptions of any training you might be considering. Although much good work is accomplished through multicultural and diversity education, if your goal is to become an effective part of the effort to dismantle racism, you need to look for training that analyzes and challenges the systemic nature of racism directly.

More general anti-oppression work—including work to dismantle sexism, classism, homophobia, and related problems—is important as well, and as a lesbian with working-class roots, I support the struggle to end these other oppressions. But anti-oppression training is not as focused as work that is specifically anti-racism, and at this point in my life, I have chosen to focus my energy, and my spiritual practice, on anti-racism.

Out of the practices of attention and education will emerge the third part of the spiritual practice of anti-racism—action. Action can be as immediate as speaking up when a racist remark or idea is expressed or as long-range as working to form an anti-racism team in your community. Since I am at the moment very much involved in learning, I can't really say where the third stage will ultimately lead me. However, I have brought together an Anti-Racism Transformation Team in my own community. More than anything else I have done in my life, this intentional effort to keep the agenda of anti-racism in the forefront of my consciousness and in the active awareness of the organizations with which I work has brought me a far distance along the way toward the wholeness I seek.

The fourth part of the spiritual practice of anti-racism, reflection, emerges naturally out of the other three. One cannot be involved in such an intense process without taking time to step back and reflect. Reflection is generally most helpful if it can be accomplished in a nonjudgmental framework—in complete honesty, without inflicting guilt. Guilt is rarely useful in bringing about change. What is important is that after (or while) engaging in action, time be taken, either alone or with colleagues, to reflect on what you are doing, evaluate your effectiveness, and allow your feelings about the process to emerge. This reflection time will undoubtedly lead you back into renewed efforts to pay attention, further education, and redefinition of the sort of action you are engaged in.

There is a sort of natural interdependence among these four aspects of the spiritual practice of anti-racism—attention, education, action, and reflection. The significance of what you are observing by paying attention will be informed by your education. What you learn through reading and training will be reinforced by paying attention. Action will be determined by what you have observed and by your education. Whatever actions you choose to engage in will be more effective because of the time you have taken to pay attention and educate yourself. And all of this will be deepened, refined, and renewed by reflection.

Having developed these practices, I doubt I will ever be without them, at least not until racism is finally eliminated! Although I have found the spiritual practice of anti-racism difficult and challenging, the benefits I have reaped are more than worth the struggle. At the very least, I have regained my sense of who I am. After years of practice, my actions are now more consistent with my principles and values. This does not mean that I never do, say, or feel anything racist; racism is still embedded in my consciousness. But because I now have the practice of paying attention, I believe I am able to learn from my mistakes. I cannot accept the idea that we are victims caught in an oppressive system that is so massive and powerful that there is nothing we can do to change things. Regaining my integrity as a person of faith and conscience, I feel empowered to make a difference in this racist world.

Perhaps of greatest value to me in my personal journey toward wholeness has been the discovery of allies and the formation of relationships of mutual commitment to work on this together. It is always good to know that we are not alone. In the spiritual practice of anti-racism, it has been most rewarding to work with those who are learning together to confront, challenge, and change the evils of racism, and to create communities that truly have the potential to bring about a future of justice and peace. For me, the vision of my earlier work for peace and justice is not dead. The first-strike nuclear weapons are finally being dismantled. And someday, with all our efforts, so will racism.

Simple Living

Ken Brown

"Simplicity, simplicity, simplicity!" wrote Henry David Thoreau more than a century ago. "I say, let your affairs be as two or three, and not a hundred or a thousand; instead of a million count half a dozen, and keep your accounts on your thumbnail."

Thoreau's words, first published in 1854, ring true for the increasing number of people striving for a more simple way of living today. They come from *Walden,* Thoreau's account of living simply on Walden Pond in Concord, Massachusetts, for slightly more than two years. Thoreau speaks to a deep yearning in many of us to live close to the wild, to be self-sufficient, and to be, in a most positive sense, free.

As a Unitarian Universalist minister, I have continually struggled to achieve a balance between the prophetic and the spiritual. In recent years I have come to see a simpler life as key to this balance. My practice is still evolving, yet simple living as part of an ongoing spiritual discipline has already changed my perspective for the better. I would like to share with you some of what has helped me move toward a spiritual discipline of simple living.

To begin, we need to talk about what simple living does not mean. In this century, Richard Gregg is credited with coining the phrase *voluntary simplicity* in an article he first published in 1936. He wrote,

Voluntary simplicity involves both inner and outer condition. It means singleness of purpose, sincerity and honesty within, as well as avoidance of exterior clutter, of many possessions irrelevant to the chief purpose of life. It means an ordering and guiding of our energy and our desires, a partial restraint in some directions in order to secure greater abundance of life in other directions. It involves deliberate organization of life for a purpose.

Too often, when we think of simple living, we think only of giving things up. Yet neither Thoreau nor Gregg speaks of it in that manner. Simple living isn't about ridding oneself of things, as much as recognizing what is important and vital to your life. One of simplicity's greatest practitioners, Mahatma Gandhi, had a similarly broad view. "Civilization, in the real sense of the term, consists not in multiplication, but in the deliberate and voluntary reduction of wants. This alone promotes real happiness and contentment."

Still, looking at our patterns of accumulation is usually part of simple living. When I began to think about this issue, I realized that, like many people, I had become accustomed to buying without thinking, which led to having more than I really require. Cutting down on possessions has been difficult, though holding large garage sales or donating many items to church rummage sales remain options for doing so in the future. More important, to me, is making intentional choices about what we accumulate in the future, and being aware of how things affect our spirits.

Clearly, those things don't bring happiness. Yet, too often, our career choices seem to support a lifestyle of accumulation. Simple living requires us to make intentional decisions about what we wish to do with our lives. For my life partner, Tommie, and me, this recently meant taking a close look at what was important for us as we enter our fifties. We realized that we needed to make some changes. Tommie sought a less stressful, equally creative job; I needed a smaller congregation in a community that offered me opportunity to be near the mountains and the ocean, to have a garden, and to develop a style of shared ministry with a congregation. We were lucky to find such opportunities to begin the next stage of our life. The process of discernment will continue, but I feel as though I've made some intentional decisions that are leading in the right direction.

Perhaps the most difficult part of simple living is making intentional decisions about what you really, truly want in your life. It requires setting goals for yourself. I do many workshops for congregations who want to plan for the future, so I know how hard it is, individually and together, to set goals. But to create a truly happy life for ourselves and our families, we need to do so. That means making choices, and letting go of those things that we might have hung on to because at some point we learned that a successful parent or a good worker did such things.

Duane Elgin, author of the 1981 book *Voluntary Simplicity: Toward a Way of Life That Is Outwardly Simple, Inwardly Rich,* is looked to as one of the gurus of the voluntary simplicity movement in our time. In his latest book *The Awakening Earth: Exploring the Evolution of Human Culture and Consciousness,* he writes that our most important priority is the creation of "compelling visions of a sustainable future. We cannot consciously build a world that we have not imagined."

A decision to move toward a simpler lifestyle means breaking the cycle at some point—making an intentional decision, imagining a different possibility for the future. It also means being able to define what living simply means to you and your family. For Thoreau, that meant living in a one-room cabin next to a pond. For today's families, it can mean leaving the city, or living off a small amount of income from work or investments. For me, it has meant changing jobs and making more intentional choices about possessions. It also means raising and eating my own vegetables, which, in addition to allowing me to live more simply, gives me an opportunity to meditate and to connect to the earth. Another aspect of simple living was to found, with Carol Benson

Holst and others, Seeds of Simplicity, a project to help parents and children find their own patterns of simple living.

Moving to a simpler lifestyle means making an intentional decision, but it must be your own decision, and your own definition. As Richard Gregg wrote, "As different people have different purposes in life, what is relevant to the purpose of one person might not be relevant to the purpose of another. . . . The degree of simplification is a matter for each individual to settle for [her- or] himself."

The point of striving to live more simply is not to become caught in a holier-than-thou approach, not to strive to copy someone else, but to make intentional decisions that feel right for you. Your spiritual practice of simple living doesn't need to fit anyone else's definition.

As Henry David Thoreau wrote, "The price of anything is the amount of life you pay for it." Do the pieces of your life fit together? Are you living the way you wish to live, not the way you think you have to live? Do you have a compelling vision of a joyous future for yourself and your family? Is the price of this future worth the amount of your life that it will take to pay for it? These are some of the questions the spiritual discipline of simple living asks of us. You have the power to make the choices that seem right for you. My experience tells me it's worth the struggle. The choice is yours.

Recycling

Audrey W. Vincent

For me, recycling has become a way of life. It has changed my buying habits, which has influenced my saving habits. It has influenced my eating habits and how I perceive myself in the interdependent web of all existence. Recycling could have been just another chore, but it has helped me cultivate an attitude that nudges me beyond the nitty-gritty of bagging newspapers, collecting cardboard and paper, and sorting aluminum, tin, glass, and plastic. Recognizing resistance and moving beyond it, I realize that through such work and discipline, I exercise my power in everyday choices in everyday places. Even in the supermarket, buying for my household, I can be attentive and reflective.

The voice that tells me not to bother, that recycling is trivia, that there are more important things I should be doing, is strong. It reflects mainstream culture, which promotes instant gratification and throwing things away when they no longer gratify us. Recyclers push against this norm. Like the demands of the everyday that pop into our minds as we settle into meditation, this voice needs to be acknowledged so that it does not dominate. My lifeline voice, the voice connecting me to the interdependent web of all existence, replies, "Yes, it may be a trivial act for one to do, but I am not one; I am not alone. Therefore, what I do is not trivial."

The reminder that I am not alone, that legions of individuals are doing similar acts all over the globe, empowers me to go on saving, sorting, and disposing of properly. I also try to reduce my use of services that pick up and dump trash at landfills, those human-made sores on the Earth's skin we have created for the burial of our discards, and to buy only items that can be recycled, renewed, or reused. In the supermarket, I ask myself: "Do I really want or need this?" If the item comes in a plastic container that is not a "1" or a "2," the only kinds of plastic recyclable in my area, how will I dispose of it after the contents are consumed? Do I really want to assume the responsibility for its disposal? Saying no to this last question usually diminishes my desire for the item and it often goes unbought, and the flotsam and jetsam in my wake here on earth are lessened.

Life feeds on life; it does not feed on plastic. The amount of plastics in our streams and oceans is beyond our worst imaginings. A beaked whale, a species never found in the waters directly off the East Coast, is found beached on a coastal barrier island. Scientists discover its stomach and half of its esophagus impacted with plastic. This animal usually feeds on squid, in very deep waters, far, far from the coast, in remote areas of the ocean. For some reason this particular animal was feeding on the surface at the rip line where the Gulf Stream meets colder currents, where vegetation and floating garbage collect. Stretching for miles out into the Atlantic, the rip line is normally a good feeding site for all kinds of fish and whales, but in recent years, the rip line has spawned an immense trough of plastic throw-aways and other materials that now reach into the remotest, deepest areas, plastics that are ingested along with plankton and fish containing ingested plastics.

I wonder what is it like to die from plastic. How do we count the loss of that which we have not seen, have not discovered washed up on shore? How do we measure sea life degradation? It is not just the death of one magnificent creature and all those we do not know about that I mourn, but also the degradation of these creatures' homes. Where once the beaked whale and other sea life swam free, they are free no longer. I make a vow to tell the whale's story to one per-

son a week and to reuse the plastic bags I bring vegetables
and fruits home in. When the last of the contents are used,
I shake out the bags and let them dry out before placing
them in cloth bags ready for the next visit to the market.

Some years ago, I saw a television documentary about a
nun in Ohio who was building her new home almost solely
from materials that had been recycled or salvaged. She began with what had been a chicken coop and added on rooms.
With the help of other sisters, neighbors, and friends, she
finished the work in days. The cost, including land and
chicken coop, was a few thousand dollars. This was a well-
insulated home, fit for midwestern winters.

The home caught my attention, but even more compelling was the sister's attitude and how she put her theology
into practice. She spoke caringly of the stuff of which her
home was made. Discarded, once-separate objects without
visible worth were redeemed through the recycling process;
their intrinsic value was restored, and they were integrated into
a structure that provides her shelter through hands-on work. A
believer in transformation, she created her home as a visible
manifestation of the theology that she lives out every day.

The nun also spoke of glass as a natural miracle. The
elements for its making are all around us in sand and silica.
The sister claimed the average life of a glass container is
thirty-nine returns and refills. She urged glass usage over
aluminum and plastic, because aluminum is a limited resource and plastic requires a more complex recycling process that pollutes. Glass is simply melted down and reshaped.
Ever since, I have valued glass as Earth's mirror of beauty
that, thanks to human ingenuity, serves us in so many practical ways. It is my preference for purchase unless safety is
an issue.

The simple things we recycle are remarkable in their own
right beyond the purposes they serve. They are both testi-
mony to nature's bounty all around us and to human ingenuity in creating uses for them beyond their natural state.
Recycling gives me opportunity to pause in my hurried sched-

ule to be wowed by their existence and to experience gratitude for their presence.

Getting started with recycling is simple once you develop
a system. Working out a system is a must, so that you do
not feel overwhelmed by the stuff you are collecting. First
find out how recycling is done in your area. Is there a city
pick-up for recyclables? When? Where are other agencies or
businesses that accept items that the city does not process?
What are their hours? Are there any sites within your line of
frequent travel? Figure out the quickest, easiest way to drop
off recyclables going to or from your work so that you do
not come to see recycling as an extra, a frill to be done only
after everything else is done. You will also need to find space
in your home, garage, or patio where you can collect and
sort items.

These details may seem tedious and mindless, but they
can add up to pleasant surprises. On some weeks, the amount
of trash I bag for the garbage pickup is diminished by more
than half. There is a mantra I say from time to time that
keeps the doing of the chores in perspective. It goes like this:
Glass, tin, plastic, and paper. You have added to my life;
now I will add to yours. Go with my blessing.

Life is a process; the universe is in process; I am in process. I want to do what I can to move the process along.
Through recycling, I do.

Vegetarianism

Helena P. Chapin

I am quite sure that the seeds for vegetarianism, my spiritual practice, were planted when I was young. I spent a great deal of time on my horse, in fields and woods, with few neighbors around. By the time I was ten, I had my own wildflower garden, full of carefully transplanted gems from the surrounding countryside. My father loved dogs, so we raised Golden Retriever puppies, while helping to deliver I don't know how many litters of kittens. As an adult, raising a family became my focus, but, gradually over the years, without realizing it, I have returned to my life of connection with animals and the earth.

When I was searching for a house four years ago, I found one with a spruce tree in front and a large cherry in back and a bare backyard in which to plant a Native American perennial flower garden. As the nursery workers promised, butterflies and birds are now my companions as I work among the flowers. This type of gardening requires composting, of course, and my vegan diet means I can use all the waste from my eating in an earth-enhancing way.

But this is getting ahead of myself. In 1991, while attending a conference, I came upon *Diet for a New America* by John Robbins. Reading that book brought back my sense of closeness to nature and animals and convinced me to begin eating a plant-based—vegan—diet as a daily reminder of this connection. I was horrified by Robbins's descriptions of the cruel and violent human behavior in our present-day food factories. Today, with few exceptions, chickens, pigs, and cows are considered to be here on earth only for human use and convenience, which often means that they endure terrible torture in the name of efficiency. There is no longer any sense of these animals being fellow creatures of this earth, no sense that the violence toward them is violence toward all life.

There are other compelling reasons to eat a plant-based diet. The raising of livestock contributes to environmental damage and resource depletion. The grain and land devoted to producing beef and other meats are not available for raising plants, which could feed the world's neediest people. Finally, a low-fat plant-based diet is healthy for the human body, having been shown to prevent or to aid in healing many diseases. I have noticed that my diet is very similar to those prescribed for heart patients.

Eating a plant-based diet may make good sense, but it is not easy. In particular, food is a very emotional issue. People are fiercely protective of their eating habits and sometimes resent those who make different choices. Even organizations like Greenpeace refrain from discussing food choices as important to the protection of the environment because people will not contribute funds to a cause that asks them to change their diets. "EARTHSAVE, Healthy People, Healthy Planet," founded by John Robbins, is the only environmental organization that links our food choices to the destruction of the earth.

Still, eating a vegan diet has become part of a satisfying spiritual practice for me. Part of this lifestyle is an attempt to live more according to the rhythms of nature. On a good morning, I rise with the sun, walk my dog, and begin to prepare my meals for the day. If I were cooking meals for a family, the additional time spent in meal preparation might not feel so life enhancing, but I live alone and find chopping and cooking healthy plant food to be a quieting experience, connecting me to the life forces of the natural environment. Also, recycling by composting means that my flowers and I share the same nourishment. Especially when I follow the meal preparation with slow dining in a favorite setting, there comes a mood of contemplation, of pondering life's gifts, of being grateful to be alive. In his book, *Care of the Soul,* Thomas Moore states that "all eating is communion, feeding the soul as well as the body. Our cultural habit of eating 'fast food' reflects our current belief that all we need to take into ourselves, both literally and figuratively, is plain food, not food of real substance, and not the imagination of real dining."

In a later book, *The Re-Enchantment of Everyday Life,* Moore states that "it's no accident that in our disenchanted times we have found hundreds of ways to short-circuit the production, preparation, and eating of food, and so it makes sense that to re-enchant our ordinary lives we could approach the supermarket, the kitchen, and the dining room differently, realizing that the extra time real food demands of us is not wasted but serves the soul." I have found this to be so.

So, how does one begin the spiritual practice of eating a vegan diet? It depends on your personality. Once I made the decision, I did it immediately. Others with whom I have talked did it gradually—giving up beef first, then chicken, then fish, then dairy—and some stopped after giving up only beef. Any reduction of meat eating will be a plus for your health, the environment, world hunger, and the treatment of animals. See the resource section of this book for information on cookbooks that I have found inspiring and helpful.

What is important, in the end, is that each of us find some way to live with a depth of appreciation for our gift of life. To better serve the natural world—and therefore, the human world—is my daily effort. Even though it is often unpopular, the spiritual practice of vegetarianism has brought me peace of mind, better health, and a sense of interdependence with our earth and its creatures.

Giving

Tony Larsen

Money is one of those things that a lot of us have trouble with. We don't want to seem materialistic, but we don't quite want to be ascetics either.

The struggle, I believe, is essentially a spiritual one. Some say we should just admit that we like having money, instead of pretending to feel guilty about it. (Someone once said, "Whoever said money can't buy happiness didn't know where to shop.") Others quote the Bible and say, "Money is the root of all evil." However, the Bible doesn't actually say that. It says "The love of money is the root of all evil" (I Timothy 6:10). It's not money itself—it's being overly attached to it. (Besides, the Bible also says, "Bread is made for laughter, and wine gladdens life—but money answers all things." Ecclesiastes 10:19 goes a little farther than I'd want to!)

My own belief is that money is neutral, neither good nor bad in itself. But it can be a tool—a vehicle, a means—to a spiritual purpose.

WHY I STARTED GIVING AS A SPIRITUAL PRACTICE

Charitable giving has been a spiritual discipline of mine for more than twenty years now. What got me started was learning about world hunger and poverty as a young adult. I read about overpopulation, I heard about the plagues of preventable diseases, I saw the starving children on TV—and I felt I needed to help. If I had never known about the problems of the world, I could have lived a fairly comfortable life. But once I witnessed them, that was no longer possible for me.

You may remember the comedian Flip Wilson, who was once asked what his religion was. He said, "I'm a Jehovah's Bystander."

The person who asked him said, "You're a *what?*"

And he said, "I'm a Jehovah's Bystander. They asked me to witness, but I didn't want to get involved."

Well, once you're a witness, you have no choice but to get involved! So when I first became aware of world hunger, I made a decision that, once I started making a decent salary I would give a significant portion of it to charities that I believed in. I have been able to do this partly because I have no children to support and partly because I had no debt to pay when I graduated from seminary. But although these factors make it possible for me to give away a higher percentage of my income than many others could, I still believe most middle-class people could give at least ten or twenty percent of their net income to charity—if they really put their minds to it.

It's not easy, of course—but it may not be as hard as you think.

HOW MUCH MONEY DO I NEED TO BE HAPPY?

The trick, at least for me, is to know that there's no particular amount of money I need in order to be happy. When people in surveys are asked how much it would take to make them happy, almost everyone says: "A little more than I have now." People who make $20,000 a year say, "If I could just make $30,000, that would take care of my bills and give me a little breathing room."

And people who make $30,000 say, "If I could just make $40,000, that would be just enough." And so on.

We all think a little more money can make us happier. And in some cases, no doubt, it would. (At least it might cut down on some of the stresses we have.) But after a while, we'd get used to the new amount and then we'd want a little more. No fixed amount would really make us happy. Howard Hughes, as you know, was a billionaire. In fact, he was the richest man in the world when he was alive. But he died of malnutrition. Money didn't do much for him.

Once you understand that no particular amount of money can make you happy, it becomes easier to live on less than you presently earn. I think of the well-to-do family who moved right next door to an Amish community. The Amish watched them unload the computer, the large-screen TV, the stereo equipment, the VCR, the Jacuzzi. To be polite, one Amish woman came over and said, "If you ever have trouble with any of those, let me know, I'd be glad to help." The new neighbor was surprised and said, "Thank you! You really know how to fix these things?" And the Amish woman replied, "No, but I'll teach you how to live without them."

HOW TO DO IT?

At any rate, this is how I live on less than I earn. Each month, when I get my paycheck, I put my designated percentage into a charity account. I then think of the income I have left as my real income—for food, bills, house payments, spending money. Then, as charitable requests come my way during the year, I donate to them out of the charity fund. At the end of the year I divide up the funds remaining in the account, so that I can start over the next year. Sometime in that next year I will get my income tax refund in the mail. When I do, I will give the same designated percentage of that amount to charity. So my charitable giving is always a percentage of net income—that is, a percentage of what I actually get. This is easier for me than taking a percentage of gross income, since taxes can vary from year to year and make it difficult to save a constant amount.

One of the benefits of planning your charitable giving this way is that you never have to feel guilty when someone asks you for a donation. You see, once you have decided on your percentage, then it's never a question of whether you'll be generous but of who needs your money more. So when you get a request to donate to the firefighters' pension fund, or to the disabled veterans, or to the Shriners for circus tickets for handicapped children, you don't have to feel guilty if you say no to one of these causes. Because the truth is, if you give to one of these causes, you are taking away money from other causes that you would otherwise have more money to give to. So you never have to feel stingy for turning down a charitable request—you're just being a good steward of the money you have available.

One of the reasons many people feel guilty when someone on the street asks them for a hand-out—or when they get a call from a charitable organization—is that they have not decided beforehand how much money they should give. So every time a request comes their way, they give out of guilt. This is not a good way to give. It means that whoever gets you first, gets your money, instead of the people and institutions to whom you want to give the most. If you designate a certain percentage of your income for charitable causes—a percentage that's high enough to be a sacrifice but low enough to be achievable—then you won't end up giving out of guilt. You'll give out of your fullness—and you'll give more wisely, too.

Most important, you will feel connected to the world around you—a part of the interdependent web of all existence. And that in itself is an experience of the holy.

EVERYONE A BROTHER OR SISTER

Perhaps this story from the Jewish Talmud will help you as much as it helps me. Time before time, when the world was young, two brothers shared a field and a mill. Each night they divided the grain they had grown together evenly. One brother lived alone, and the other had a large family. Now, the single brother thought to himself one day, "It isn't really fair that we divide the grain evenly. I have only myself to care for, but my brother has children to feed." So each night he secretly took some of his grain and put it in his brother's granary. But the married brother said to himself one day, "It isn't fair that we divide the grain evenly—because I have children to provide for me in my old age, but my brother doesn't." So *he* began every night to take some of *his* grain and put it in his brother's granary. Then, one night, they met each other halfway between their two houses, and they realized what had been happening. And then, what could they do but embrace each other in love? The legend is that God witnessed their meeting and proclaimed: "This is a holy place. And here it is that my temple shall be built." And so it was that the first temple was constructed in Jerusalem.

If we understand that everyone is brother and sister to us, then we will always want to pour some of our grain into the granary of the world. And when we do—and where we do—that is a holy place.

ENGAGING THE SOUL

Creativity

Quilting

Laurie Bushbaum

When I was thirteen, I inherited an unfinished quilt started by my great-grandmother. A few years later, I finished it as best I could. I used it on my bed all through high school, and it was stained and bedraggled by the time I graduated. Still, it was precious to me, so I tucked it away in a closet. Fifteen years later I painstakingly took it apart, stitch by stitch, to salvage a few of the squares that were in better condition. I wanted to use these squares in a new quilt I was making called "Four Generations Handed Down," in which I honored my creative genealogy, four generations of textile artists in my family.

In the process of finishing that first quilt from my great-grandmother, and the many that have followed, I discovered that quilting can be a powerful metaphor for the spiritual life on both the personal and collective levels. Each of us has the task of taking the scraps of our lives, the beautiful satins and velvets, the plain everyday calicoes, the bumpy corduroys, the dark shades as well as the bright, and making them into a thing of unique beauty. It is a neverending project. At times it is too much to do alone. The old quilting bees remind us of that; the women gathered together, sometimes for days at a time, sharing their food, their stories, their families and lives, all the while stitching, stitching.

Eventually, quilting became more than a metaphor, but it took me many years to finally name and claim my spiritual discipline. Along the way I tried Transcendental and other forms of meditation. I have tried various forms of prayer. I have tried the Zen of jogging and vegetarianism. I have renounced formalized religion and become a minister. Each of these practices has been a useful teacher on the path, but none of them is the path itself. But quilting is my spiritual discipline, my prayer and meditation. Needle through thread, up and down, is my rosary, my mantra. It is my path to comfort, clearer understanding, and renewed compassion for the world.

But recognizing my spiritual discipline did not come easily to me. All of my life the two driving forces of my spirit have been art and the spiritual life. I faced several obstacles in learning how absolutely central and connected the two are for me. For example, when I was in elementary school and in 4-H club, sewing was one of my projects. Part of the annual judging for the sewing students was to model the garment you made. The judges always asked where you planned to wear your creation. The girls who made the proverbial navy blue polyester dress with peter-pan collar replied, "Church." The denim jumper was for "school." What did I say about my black velvet and wild print, anklelength gypsy dress that laced up the front? Even as a child, working with fabric was not primarily a way to expand my wardrobe, but a way to explore my mind and spirit. 4-H didn't have a category for that.

Another stumbling block I faced in naming my spiritual discipline had to do with the values of the art world. In college, I remember standing outside the art building having been told by a faculty member that I could not do an independent study in quilting because there was no faculty member who could supervise such a class. And though quilting might be interesting, it was not real art and didn't belong in the department. I was stunned and confused.

In seminary, I was excited by the ideas and words of several theologians in particular, but I was also drowning in words. I longed for another way to explore what I didn't know about the life of the spirit and to express what I did know. I longed for a hands-on way to pray, to enter into the Mystery. I was drawn to religious art of many kinds, but I knew that I was not a Russian Orthodox icon painter, a Shaker furniture maker, or a practitioner of Japanese ikebana (flower arranging). The quilts of the Amish spoke deeply to me, but quilting then was still an extracurricular activity for me and I didn't have time in seminary life to do what I most needed.

Slowly, I have come to understand that quilting for me is about worship. The word *worship* comes from an old word meaning, "to shape things of worth." One aspect of worship is transformation, transforming the ordinary into the Sacred, the remnant into the Holy. For me, quilting as spiritual discipline is giving shape and color and texture to my inner life. It is about making beauty from what is at hand.

Whatever else art may be, it is primarily work of the soul. When I talk about art I am not talking about art in the modern, Western way that makes it into either an activity for the exclusively gifted or into a consumer item. Art is very much a sacrament, an outward and visible sign of inward and spiritual grace. Art is not so much what we make, but how we relate to the world. Not a noun, but a verb. This puts art back in a position to be claimed by the many. Quilting has been a way for me to use a particular discipline as a means of discovering that it is not the art creation itself that matters so much but what the process of creation teaches.

What has the spiritual discipline of quilting taught me? First, it has taught me the beauty and necessity of pattern. Pattern is a fundamental part of our human experience, as basic as day and night, as complex as theology and mathematics. My four-year-old was suddenly taken with the idea of pattern one night when we sat at the kitchen table and snack time turned into a profound experience in recognizing and making pattern. Long skinny pretzels interspersed with Cheerios can make an infinite number of patterns. Then, suddenly, there were patterns not just in the snacks, but on the kitchen tile, the wallpaper, and in the order of our days.

My son's mind was alight with revelation; he grasped pattern as a way of marking time and space, inner as well as outer. Pattern is the background against which we can see Revelation, with which we can balance constancy with change. Spiritual discipline is knowing and recognizing the patterns in one's self, changing them if necessary and possible, tuning one's self to the larger cosmic patterns, and gracefully resting in this beauty.

Quilting has taught me to respect the wisdom of the elders, of paying attention to early lessons. For many years I made traditional quilts. It was all I knew. I delighted in being part of this communion of saints, women (and a few men) who through time have made beauty out of next to nothing. After several years, though, I hit a wall. I was suddenly bored. I didn't want to follow anybody else's pattern. I had mastered all the basic skills, but needed a new way to use them.

And that is the next thing that this spiritual discipline taught me—to take risks, to listen to the still small voice urging me into new territory. Creation always involves risk, whether it be the creation of a new piece of artwork, a new recipe, a new relationship. Many of my pieces have started out with a certain plan only to end up quite different than I imagined. Sometimes I have tried one color of fabric in a particular spot and ripped it out the next day. Even the quilts that I did many years ago that are no longer exciting to me are a visual testament to my journey, my deepening understanding, my growing experience and wisdom.

The spiritual discipline of quilting has also taught me the rhythms of the creation process. Many of my quilt pieces were started, partially completed, only then to spend two or three years on a shelf waiting for the vision to reappear or clarify. I used to panic thinking the piece was a throw-away. Or I would fight the fallow time and try to force the resolution. Slowly I have learned the wisdom of letting these things happen when the time is right. When the inspiration comes, it sometimes comes with such dazzling, simple clarity that I can only say a quiet "Thank you" for this amazing grace.

And this knowledge transfers over to my sermon writing. I have learned that my sermon writing also has a very particular pattern. Now, when I hit the wall in my writing, I know to do a load of laundry or a stack of filing or to wash the dishes. If I allow these seemingly empty spaces, the pregnant pauses, yet pay careful attention, the sermon does get finished.

When I am in my studio, I can forget my name, the time, the needs of my children, the tasks on my list of things to do. This is one of the benefits of spiritual discipline—to be immersed in Holy Time, dissolved in Sacred Space. When I fully enter the work, I return refreshed, invigorated, as if I had traveled to a new land. I can return to my daily tasks with greater joy and deeper presence. The opposite is true, too. When I can't find time in my life for my creative soul work, it is hard for me to give to the world around me what I would like to give. For years I struggled, thinking that my artwork was selfish. Then I noticed the profound effects it has on everything else that I do. Though I quilt for myself, I have come to understand it as a necessary form of spiritual renewal, a way to fill my cup so that I may fill others'.

The most recent gift of my spiritual discipline is discovering that it can also be a gift for others. Only in the last few years have I begun to show my pieces in galleries and churches. I am amazed by what others tell me they see or feel from the pieces. The quilts invite contemplation, incite feelings of peace and hope, allow one to revel in beauty. Some very small, private image that I think I have tucked away in a corner often jumps out for others and speaks to their spirits, too. Sometimes I have done something in a quilt piece totally unconsciously, only to have a viewer walk up to it and immediately point out what was too close for me to see. It is both humbling and exciting to speak to another's spirit and heart without words, to be reminded that there is a language of image and color and texture.

The requirements to begin quilting are very minimal: a needle, thread, some fabric. Since the art of quilting is experiencing a revival of interest, books abound. Many towns and cities have quilting groups. The easiest place to find out about them is your local general fabric store or a quilting store if there is one near you. Even if you live in an isolated area, there are mail order resources available. *Quilters Newsletter Magazine* is great for beginners and traditional quilters. For those who want to see the cutting edge of the craft, *Art/Quilt Magazine* (P.O. Box 630927, Houston, TX) will delight you beyond imagining.

By simple definition, quilting is merely sewing pieces of fabric together into a whole. But as spiritual discipline, it is a careful attention to the details of my life. Quilting as spiritual discipline is entering the sensual richness of the universe, creating order out of chaos, beauty out of the simple, wholeness from the scraps, and in the midst, being transformed.

Meditation by Hand

L. Annie Foerster

Needlepointing, the drawing of pictures in wool on a canvas ground, has been, for me, a spiritual practice not unlike meditation. The cadence of the needle entering and exiting the canvas is a soothing heartbeat, releasing me from my own body. The wool yarn is a tactile reflection, rough and strong, tying me to the physical world. The sensuous colors are as healing as a rainbow, weaving in and out of the mesh, evoking the spiritual dimension. The varied patterns and pictures that emerge are silent witnesses to the act of co-creation. The discipline of needlepointing, like the practice of staring at a candle or counting breaths, focuses the mind, making it more perceptive, less scattered.

I often took a segment of needlepointing with me to meetings. I discovered I was more attentive, less likely to interrupt another speaker, more thoughtful in my own responses. The steady rhythm of the work kept my mind steady as well, kept me from jumping to conclusions or misunderstanding another point of view.

I practiced needlepoint meditation for several years while my life was going satisfactorily, emerging day by day as smooth and rhythmical as the needlepointing itself. Then I found myself enmeshed in a temporary crisis, tripped by a bump in my life, a predicament that would require much time to resolve. Just when I might have needed their comfort most, I found it difficult to take up my needle and yarns. Needlepointing no longer soothed me; it didn't focus my thoughts or give me pleasure. In fact, working on it disturbed me. So much for needlepointing as a meditation, I told myself. Spiritual disciplines should sustain you in bad times as well as good.

I put my needlepointing away. At meetings, my restless fingers beat tattoos on the table. With nothing in them, my empty hands attempted to console one another, but the massaging of one by the other in turn brought no peace of mind, no spiritual satisfaction. My body, restless and fidgety, reflected the feverish activity of my brain, which was seeking a solution to my problems, turning over impossible resolutions, never at rest.

I continued a practice of silent meditation twice a day, a discipline that gave me some courage and the incentive to plough through the storms of crisis and the mudslides of everyday life. But I missed the spiritual grounding that needlework had given me.

One day, confronted with a block of free time, I felt called to begin a quilt. I gave in to the unfamiliar urge and began to cut and arrange pieces of cloth. The fragmented scraps reflected my disjointed thinking; the mess I made flinging cottons about the sewing table matched the messiness of my present life. Once begun, the project became an obsession. Every free moment I could find was spent in the sewing room, cutting and piecing, laying out designs and fitting them together like a puzzle. Twenty-seven different fabrics found their way into the emerging pattern; hundreds of tiny pieces, some no more than half an inch wide, were cut and sewn together. I hurled fabric and threads about in a frenzy of activity that allowed no negative thoughts to break through while I worked, no despair, no doubts, no judgments. Somewhere along the way I decided I would wear this quilt, rather than lay it on a bed. I carved it into a jacket.

On the day I held up the completed garment, I felt a familiar sense of peace. I was as calm as I had been when I was needlepointing, as whole as when my life was not burdened by conflict. A voice within me spoke the wisdom I needed to hear: You can make order out of chaos! And I knew it was as true of my life as it was of the quilted jacket I had just completed.

The predicaments that disrupted my life lasted for nearly three years and in that time I made eight pieced jackets! Always as I stitched, I had an intuitive feeling that where chaos exists, it need not control. Now when I left the sewing room, I no longer twitched or fretted. I had discovered another form of creative meditation. I had confirmed that creativity—a meditation by hand—can be a spiritual discipline.

While standard spiritual disciplines are always worth exploring and practicing, I have discovered that creative activities, practiced with intentionality and without concern for outcome or gain, are as evocative of the spirit as the more traditional ones. Whether it be journal-writing or poetry, handcrafts or music-making, there is a creative activity that speaks to every soul, and a practice that has the power to heal and strengthen it.

Your creative practice can be tailored to the needs of your life. For me, needlepointing had been a social meditation, one I could do in company, one that would help me listen attentively, but not get in the way of my participation. What I needed during the crisis were periods of solitude, withdrawal for my own sake and the sake of my relationships. Cutting and sewing requires a dedicated space and more room than your lap, so while I was piecing and quilting, I was forced to be alone, allowed to turn inward, focus on my own thoughts and healing.

I have discovered some guidelines as I have experimented with meditation by hand—with spiritual creativity:

While you practice the creative art you have chosen as your meditation, try not to be concerned with how much you have accomplished or how much there is to be done. Stay in the moment of creation—let it fill you and feed you. Let yourself feel the colors, hear the sounds, discover the meanings of whatever medium you select. As your creation is a part of yourself, allow yourself to be a part of your creation. That is soul work.

Be excellent—as good as you can be—in your practice, but do not judge the outcome or product. This sounds like a paradox and requires great patience and practice to achieve, for we tend to equate our own worth with false comparisons or become disgusted with our mistakes. Make the ripping out of inaccuracies—the erasing of words or the remolding of clay—be as creative as the rest of the process. There is a joy in such re-creating, when impatience is banished; there is a discipline that is delicious and deepening.

Allow yourself to choose a new medium when the one you are practicing is not right for a particular moment in your life, or let a new medium choose you. Intuition is part of the creative process. Go so far as to put away an unfinished project in order to start a new one. One day it will be right to return to it.

Your creation will let you know when it is finished if you listen with your heart. When we decide with our heads, we often stop too soon or carry it too far. When that completion occurs, celebrate it: Display it, wear it, sing it, share it, give it away. This celebration is part of the spiritual practice—a way to honor your creative spirit without arrogance or judgment.

Creativity requires imagination and faith, a belief that what can be imagined is possible. An ancient wisdom suggests that while food is necessary for life, we can live for weeks without food; while water is necessary for life, we can live for days without water; and while breath is necessary for life, we can live for several minutes without breath. But if one has no creative imagination, one might as well be dead. Why not practice a spiritual discipline that encourages life?

Gardening

Barbara Davenport

All I Really Need to Know I Learned in Kindergarten, Robert Fulghum called his book. For me, all I really need to know I learned in the garden. Tending a garden from clearing to planting to harvesting has been my way of cultivating the soul.

My hands and heart have dwelt in some patch of dirt every year of my life; gardening has nourished this body and soul for all of its fifty-seven years. Nature's gifts—dirt, seeds, sun, and rain—combine to sustain life. These are gifts many of us take for granted, gifts we cannot create, gifts I hope we will not destroy.

I grew up on a 140-acre farm in rural Vermont, a sort of Noah's ark with pairs of goats, sheep, cows, ducks, pigs, horses, and a two-acre vegetable garden. Providence and the work of our hands provided all that we ate. I grew up in the garden and lived by its seasons.

When I was young, my parents did most of the actual work of gardening. Standing close to my parents with small helping hands outstretched, I listened and learned.

Gardens are nature's classroom: a place to encourage children's imagination; a place to instill a love of plants and all of nature; a place to learn the value of work and its rewards. A failed crop can be a perfect opportunity to explain the life cycle through which all living things travel. One of my favorite definitions of God comes from a child in a Sunday school class who said, "God is what knows how to grow." By participating in gardening, children learn that they constitute, with all growing things, a single community of life. They learn to nurture, and to be nurtured, in a universe that is often uncertain but ultimately beneficent. Young hands and hearts are guided on their own journeys from the gardens of their parents to ones of their own making by the god of the garden.

Kneeling beside Gramma Davenport, listening as she hummed her favorite hymns like "Rock of Ages," with my six-year-old hands pulling weeds, I knew I was in church. God was present, guiding the growing in this garden, nature's cathedral of the world.

As I grew older I took more responsibility. So too with my spiritual growth and development. First wise elders guided my path. Later I became the hopeful gardener of my own soul, feeding and weeding my own inner spirit. In our gardens we learn the deepest of spiritual lessons. Gardening teaches me just about every lesson I need for living.

GARDENING TEACHES US HOW WE ARE LINKED TO THE LAND

The most ancient religious rituals arise from the agricultural seasons: spring's promise of new life and growth, summer's sunny abundance, autumn's gathering in, and winter's deep and dark waiting. By participating in the direct preparation of our own food in collaboration with nature, we understand our true link to the land upon which our survival depends.

For Vermont children in the 1940s, spring vacation from school coincided with "sugaring off," a time not set by our fixed calendar of today, but by thawing days and freezing nights. The changes in temperature cause the sap of the sugar maple tree to rise up from its roots in the day, and descend at night, thereby filling buckets of slightly sweet water which, when repeatedly boiled down, provided the only sugar I knew as a child and which remains my favorite sweet.

Not only did whole families collect buckets of sap, but those same families also celebrated maple sugar festivals at church. "Sugar on snow" suppers were, and still are, the event of the season in rural Vermont. We would eat franks and beans (which really served as side dishes to the main course), fresh, hot maple syrup drizzled over tin pie plates of mounded snow, dill pickles (to cut the sweetness), and homemade cake doughnuts for a filler. The biggest controversy at these sugar-on-snow church suppers (discussed with all the fervor of the grandest theological debate) was the correct order in which to eat pickle, doughnut, and syrup.

Linked to the land in this way, we more clearly understand the meaning of these familiar words: "For everything there is a season and a time for every matter under heaven: a time to be born, and a time to die; a time to plant and a time to pluck up what is planted" (Ecclesiastes 3:1-2 RSV). The hand of God connects spring and fall, seed and harvest with all the seasons of our souls. We change and grow with each season.

The god of the garden is a god for all seasons. The god of the garden is what knows how to grow.

GARDENING TEACHES US SELF-REFLECTION

Gardens are mirrors of our souls through which we can see clearly into ourselves.

My neighbor's pea plants are taller than mine, and it's killing me! The competitive spirit has no place in the garden, but I feel it anyway. Then I feel guilty for having these feelings and start questioning myself: What's wrong with my pea plants, or rather what's wrong with me? Did I plant too late, buy the wrong seeds, not provide enough compost, forget to water?

Jealousy and self-judgment are not the worst of my faults. Armed with a paring knife and salt shaker, I engage in an early morning search-and-destroy mission, patrolling the strawberry patch in "The Slug Wars." My anger and vengeance intensify with every row of baby lettuce these slimy creatures devour. On slug patrol I come right up against the most difficult of theological challenges. Who shall live? The lettuce or the slugs? This is not one of my Harvard Divinity School exam questions about the hermeneutics of eschatology. This is real war—my intention is death to the invaders of my space. Sometimes not only do I gleefully count the dead in the jar cap filled with beer, but I stab them just to make sure they are really dead. Perhaps this is what Ecclesiastes meant when he wrote: "A time to love and a time to hate, a time for war and a time for peace" (Ecclesiastes 3:8 RSV).

I am not proud of my competitive and murderous aspects. I do not always like what looks back at me from the mirror of my soul, but self-reflection is part of the process of cultivating the garden of the soul.

The god of the garden sees all and blesses all without judgment.

GARDENING TEACHES US GENEROSITY

I have never met a gardener the world over who was not generous.

Recently I returned from a month-long visit to my daughter and son-in-law, who live and teach in one of southern Africa's most impoverished countries. I brought back a gift of brightly variegated tan and purple flower seeds bestowed upon me by a gardener from Tanzania. He thought seeds from his garden at the base of snow-capped Mt. Kilimanjaro would flourish in a garden two continents away, nestled at the base of glacier-covered Mt. Baker. So this spring, I planted his passion flower seeds along with seeds I purchased from Burpee Seed Company and reflected on the contrast between Burpee's patented high-priced seeds and the gift from the African gardener. Who gave Burpee their first seeds?

Gardening cultivates generosity and gratitude for the gifts freely given. The god of the garden knows no private ownership, no power over, no permission to oppress. The god of the garden knows no east or west, no north or south.

The god of the garden blesses the generous giver.

GARDENING TEACHES US PATIENCE

In gardening, as in all of life, shortcuts and impatience do not work.

As a college student, I crammed for my English literature exams. As a result, all I remember about *War and Peace* is that it is about Russia. In gardening, you cannot cram. You cannot wait until the last minute to plant and expect a harvest the next day. Shortcuts do not work in a natural world, just as they do not work in our spiritual world. You cannot cram and suddenly become a person of integrity, courage or compassion. In relationships, caring, sharing, tenderness, and consideration can never grow and flourish when too little time is spent nurturing the seeds of shared vision, trust, and compassion. There are no shortcuts and no way to fake the harvest. One quick application of instant "Miracle-Gro" for the soul will not do. The law of the garden works as inexorably in everyday life as in nature—what we sow, we must inevitably reap.

The god of the garden blesses the patient sower and reaper.

GARDENING TEACHES US TO BELIEVE IN MIRACLES

A garden is one place in the universe in which you can see and even touch a miracle.

My compost heap is teeming with tiny, squirming, food processing plants whose work no human technology can duplicate. Dead and dying kitchen waste becomes reborn through lowly earthworms, whose life work is transforming garbage into black gold. These creatures work day and night and teach us that miracles do not just happen all at once, but often come after a lot of hard work. So too with the transformation of our souls from death to rebirth.

The god of the garden transforms the dead into the living.

GARDENING TEACHES US WONDER

Our gardens draw us into that profound, unspeakable knowledge that we are inseparable from the land we live on, connected in the web of past, present, and future generations. Corn seeds pass from one generation to another, assuring a world without end. Each one of us who supports nature's efforts is a co-creator of life. Each one of us who becomes a hopeful gardener of the soul is a co-creator of a faith that we can and will sustain ourselves.

In our gardens, we pause to wonder at the ultimate paradoxes of life. Although it is true that we reap what we sow, it is equally true that we sow what we do not reap and reap what we do not sow. When my daughter and I moved to Bellingham, Washington, three plum trees in the yard of our new house offered us the most luscious purple plums I have ever tasted. These plums grew on trees planted years ago by someone I will never know, but the fruits of whose labor I eat. These plums are truly a gift from a gardener who had faith in an unknown future.

"Even if I knew certainly the world would end tomorrow, I would plant an apple tree today," the sixteenth-century theologian Martin Luther once said. Luther understood the true meaning of the paradox of faith: Faith is belief in the unbelievable, but believing in it anyway.

The god of the garden cultivates eternal hope and faith.

GETTING STARTED AS A GARDENER OF THE SOUL

How might you start becoming a hopeful gardener of your own soul? Begin with a personal assessment of your earthly surroundings and outdoor space around you. Ask yourself, how does my plot or pot of earth reflect my character and my spiritual life? What would I like to change in the garden of my soul? What lessons might I learn from tending a garden?

Then, move from meditation to action. Begin your own garden. Help others learn gardening skills. Plant more than you need, and give the rest away. Donate land to someone without a garden plot.

In the final analysis, gardening is active participation in the deepest mysteries of the universe. Through gardening we learn that we constitute, with all growing things, a single community of life. Gardening puts us in touch with the deepest of human emotions—faith, gratitude, disappointment, patience, and hope. Gardening puts us in touch with life's greatest mystery, death and rebirth.

The god of my garden blesses each and every gardener of the soul.

Cooking

Lynn M. Brodie

I like to start my spiritual practice—cooking—with a recipe. One of my favorites goes like this: Grab a large pot, pour in two tablespoons of oil and heat it on the stove. Chop up one cup of onion and one tablespoon of fresh garlic. Throw them in the pot. Add a pile of fresh chopped basil, one heaping teaspoon of dry oregano, two bay leaves, and one and a half teaspoons of salt. Sauté them all together. Add tomatoes (1 lb., 13 oz.), tomato puree (1 lb., 13 oz.), a heaping quarter teaspoonful of black pepper, a pinch of red pepper, half a cup of fresh chopped parsley, and a little wine or beer (half a cup or so). Cook it over very low heat all day on the stove or in the crock pot. Stir it, taste it, and adjust the seasonings regularly.

When I make this recipe for tomato sauce, I'm not just getting a meal on the table. There is much more going on. To start with, I am paying close attention to all the sights, sounds, smells, and textures. I am smelling the sharp odor of garlic as I hold the cloves between my fingers and chop. I am listening to the sizzle of onions sautéing on the stove. I am watching bright red tomato puree pour from a metal can onto the sizzling spices and enjoying the contrast of color as I drop fresh green parsley on top. I am feeling myself present in the moment. Throughout the day as I go about my other work, my nostrils are filled with the warm, spicy aroma of a sauce made just the way I like it, and I am connecting with my mother, my father, my grandmothers, and all the cooks in my family going back to generations I've never met.

Like most children, I learned to cook by helping my mother in the kitchen. When my mother took out the mixer and pulled out the canisters of flour and sugar, I would run to her side. "What are you making? Can I help?" I especially liked it when she made chocolate chip cookies. I would watch the beaters smooth out the softened sticks of butter and margarine. Then I would watch her check the recipe. She would let me carefully measure the sugar using a flat metal leveler to get just the right proportions. She would check the recipe again and we would add the eggs. Then we'd carefully measure the flour, baking powder, baking soda, and salt into a separate bowl. At the end we would mix in the chocolate chips and nuts by hand. Then we would chill the dough for two hours and wait. When the dough was ready, I loved to drop lumpy spoonfuls onto the cookie sheets (and into my mouth). I'd watch my mother put them in the oven, and I'd wait for a long ten minutes. It was always thrilling when she opened the oven door with a pot holder over her hand and took out the tray. It seemed magical that those light-colored blobs of dough had become steaming, flattened, toasty brown cookies filled with melting chocolate chips. (Tasting was as good as cooking itself.)

My mother did lots of cooking: scrambled eggs, French toast, blueberry pancakes, birthday cakes from scratch, sugar cookies, meatloaf, meatballs, jams, and jellies. Some special recipes she made the way her mother had made them, like rhubarb sauce, French Canadian macaroni and cheese with tomatoes, and hamburg on toast. With those recipes came her stories of watching her mother cook and sharing meals with her own family as she grew up.

And then the day came when I could try her recipes myself. Mom started working full time when I was twelve years old. My brother, my sister, and I cooked one meal each for the family every week. I learned to make all my favorite recipes. Then I began looking for new recipes and trying them out. I had a great time chopping and stirring, mashing and frying, plunging my hands into bowls full of dough and squeezing it between my fingers. I never thought of it as spiritual, but I certainly enjoyed my cooking nights. At the end of my evenings of kitchen creation, pots and bowls and spoons lay strewn across sticky counters. No one wanted the clean-up job on those nights.

My father didn't cook much until my parents separated. Then, he plunged into it with enthusiasm. We cooked breakfast together, as well as all kinds of breads, special dinners, and barbecues with homemade French fries. Once a year we'd drive eight hours to visit his mother. I loved to watch my grandmother roll out dough and make homemade spaghetti. I was amazed the first time she asked if we wanted potato chips. She proceeded to peel and slice thin pieces of potato and fry them in oil on the stove as if that was what everyone did when they wanted potato chips. She always sent us home loaded with homemade breads and cookies.

When I moved away from home to attend college, I didn't have a kitchen, so I bought all my meals in the cafeteria. But sometimes I'd pull out my hot pot and mix up a soup concoction for a snack. When I moved to an apartment off campus, my friends talked about how they didn't bother cooking just for themselves. I never understood that. I cooked up something simple each night, and once in a while I even made a pot of meatballs or a small roast chicken. I never thought much about why I did it—I just liked to cook. Now I know why. Those were times of connection and creation. Alone in my apartment, I felt connected to my family by a tradition of cooking.

When I began seriously dating, then married and had two children, my cooking had a new focus. Cooking connects me to the people I am cooking for. I focus on creating food that will nourish the bodies and souls of my family and any company we might have. Even when they aren't helping me cook, my family is connected to the process through invisible waves of fragrant steam emerging from the kitchen.

When we sit down together in the evening and spoon a fresh-cooked meal onto our plates, we all participate in that connection to our senses, our present moment, our selves.

Creation in cooking often follows a set pattern, the recipe. But the end result differs from person to person and day to day. Each act of cooking is unique. I've reached a point in my practice of cooking in which I like to take lots of liberties. I usually don't measure exactly. I don't hesitate to substitute one ingredient for another or try leaving ingredients out. Sometimes I more or less follow a recipe, other times I invent something new. But whatever process I use emerges from my life. Recipes I choose to follow or invent are based on my past experience, on my dietary values at the time, on the ingredients available in my house or those I can afford at the store, on the way I feel and the way I wish to connect with others around me. Recipes I choose to cook always come out of the depths of who I am and where I am in life at a particular moment. All that is in me participates in the act of cooking.

But cooking is not merely an expression of myself. The process of creation shapes who I am in many ways. For example, cooking strengthens my awareness of my dependence on the earth. I like to start with basic ingredients and cook from scratch because it puts me in closer contact with the source of the food. I don't grind my flour myself, but it is easier to see the connection to wheat in a bag of whole grain flour than in a package of processed baking mix. When I use fresh herbs and vegetables from the store or from my garden, I feel the same connection.

Cooking has also been a way to connect with the mysterious process of creation. In cooking, one combines separate, individual ingredients and transforms them into something new. Line up all the ingredients for muffins: flour, baking powder, baking soda, salt, sugar, milk or yogurt, oil, fruit. Each has a unique taste and texture that is nothing like a muffin. Combine these ingredients, bake them in the oven, and the special qualities of each ingredient mix with the others. When the muffins are removed from the oven, they have become a new entity, different from each of the ingredients by themselves. This happens in a more or less dramatic fashion in all cooking.

Although I've always enjoyed it, I realized that cooking is a spiritual practice for me only recently. As a wife, a mother of two young children, a homeowner, and a dog owner, I knew I needed to streamline my life when I started attending graduate school. I knew I wouldn't have time for all the hobbies and friendships I had kept up before. I decided I would cook less often or cook less involved meals. Week after week I kept telling myself, "This is crazy, I don't have time for all this cooking." But somehow I found myself making the time to cook and being happy that I had.

Slowly, I realized why I couldn't give up cooking. Cooking was much more than a way to feed the physical bodies of my family and myself. It was much more than an enjoyable hobby. Cooking nourished my soul, too. No wonder I wasn't able (or willing) to give it up to make room for other things in my life. Like all good spiritual experience, the time spent in practice enhances the rest of life rather than taking something valuable away.

My pot of tomato sauce is a prayer that has developed and evolved over the years. As a child I sat at the kitchen table and watched my mother make tomato sauce. When I began to make sauce on my own, I followed her recipe exactly, creating a smooth, mild, flavorful sauce. I would mix up meatballs from ground beef, broil them and drop them into the sauce to cook all day, just as my mother always did.

When my parents divorced, my father showed me a new way to make spaghetti sauce, drawing on his Italian heritage. It was a spicy, chunky, and potent sauce. When it got too thick, we'd never add water as my mother did, only red wine—lots of it. We didn't bother mixing up meatballs, but fried spicy Italian sausage and mixed it in.

In college I began to cook a sauce that combined my mother and father's recipes, not as mild as my Mom's, not as hot as my Dad's. I didn't bother measuring ingredients anymore, I just added them and tasted regularly to make sure I had a good combination. When there wasn't wine around I'd dump in a can of beer.

A couple of years after I got married, my husband and I stopped eating red meat. I came up with my own recipe for ground turkey meatballs to go with our changing lifestyle. Then we stopped eating meat altogether so I came up with a vegetarian meatball that can't simmer in the sauce all day. For a year or so when my young son absolutely refused to eat any vegetables, I added grated carrot to the sauce. I'm sure the sauce, like all my cooking, will continue to evolve with the ever-changing inner and outer lives of myself and the members of my family.

When I cook I am part of the interconnecting past, present, and future of humanity. I have opened a window to my own inner soul and to the world around me. I am completely involved in the activities of life and paying close attention to all that surrounds me. By being fully present in the moment, I experience a peace, a connection, and a rootedness. Through this awareness I am connected with the ultimate forces of the universe within and without. That is my definition of spirituality. When the activities of one's life become spiritual practice in these ways, the activities of life itself become a prayer.

Art

Julie-Ann Silberman

Artwork is my daily spiritual practice. My goal is not to create masterpieces, but to get more closely in touch with my interior spiritual life. In my life, I use words a lot, I read a lot, and I think a lot. I need a spiritual practice that will take me away from those things and get me in touch with what is happening at the core of my being.

Since I was a child, artwork has been central to my self-image. I went to art classes every Saturday morning at the local community college from the time I was five until I was fifteen. I was going to grow up to be an artist. I knew it and so did everyone else. As it turns out, we were both right and wrong. I have grown up to be an artist, but it was through a painful unveiling of a deeply buried part of my soul, and it is my avocation, not my vocation. I finished an undergraduate degree in art, but in those last few years of college, my focus changed, and I decided to pursue a career in a different field. Somehow my creativity was stifled.

I don't believe that I am at all unusual. I think most people are creative and love to explore their artistic sides, but something in our culture devalues creativity. It happens in many different ways. It is the young child who wants to create wildly colorful abstractions but is encouraged to stay within the lines of the preset images in the coloring book. It is the parent who says, "That's nice, dear, but how will you make a living?" It is our peers who say it isn't cool to let out the deep inner workings of our minds and hearts through art.

There are a few lucky souls whose creativity remains unstifled, but the rest of us must learn to listen to our inner voices anew. For me, that hearing came through pain. My father died, and I was sad and lonely and wanted to express the feelings raging inside me. Telling my friends was not enough. I could feel an aching in my arms and heart. I could see images in my head, but I didn't have the time, the opportunity, or the will to let them out. I had felt those longings before my father's death, but for some reason, they had not yet become urgent enough. I needed a vehicle for the day in and day out process of grieving.

So, I returned to the tried and true longing of my body. I went into my basement and dug up some old pastels and oil paints. I put on some tattered clothes. I stretched and primed several canvases on old wood-framed screens I took from my windows. I began to remember some of the places that I had called studios when I was in college, and I realized that my basement would be fine. In fact, it was a great place to create.

For me, finding a place to be creative had always been one of the bigger stumbling blocks. I didn't want the smell of paints in the house. I didn't want to risk getting stuff on the furniture or the floor or the rug because it would take too long to clean up. I had used every excuse I could muster. Then, I saw them for what they were. If I wanted to be creative, I could be creative. Space didn't matter. Mess didn't matter. With this realization, I started to unpack old art supplies and buy new ones.

Buying new art supplies is part of the spirituality of art and one of the first steps to take in making artwork a spiritual practice. You don't have to buy the most expensive stuff, but buy supplies that excite you and that will work as a vehicle for your self-expression. I had been a painter before. I work mainly with pastels now, both chalk and oil. I have chosen pastels because I can really be a part of the work— there's no brush to create distance. The pastel is a direct link between my hand and the paper or canvas.

The next step is to put your supplies out in a place where you spend a lot of time! If you spend time at your kitchen table, put the art supplies there. If you spend time in front of the TV, put them there. Initially, you are more likely to be able to tap into the creative aspects of your everyday spirituality if you try to create in the places where you usually spend time. Eventually you may want a special place for creating, but in the early stages of developing your spiritual discipline of creation, it is important that your practice be a part of your daily existence.

For me, spirituality is not about separating myself from my life. It is about getting more deeply in touch with the sacred in my daily living. Human life is sacred; therefore, what we do and how we fill our lives is sacred. So when you are doing your ordinary things, tap into the sacred. Listen to your soul. Use that to make your art.

Don't try initially to create representational art; rather, try to use color to express your feelings. Often I begin by closing my eyes. Usually in that darkness I see colors, and I begin with what my inner eye has selected. As I continue to work, I will frequently close my eyes and explore the image in my mind's eye, how it changes and develops. It is easier to change things in your head than it is on the paper or canvas. Perceiving images guided by inner awareness is important to understanding creation as a spiritual discipline.

When I studied ceramics in college, I learned that I could not center clay with my eyes open. Instead, I had to feel the center. Similarly, art as a spiritual discipline is the chosen need to find center. While finding true center may not be as vital to technique in working with paint or pastels as it is to working with clay, finding center in an emotional sense is vital to the quality, depth, and meaning of your work, whatever the medium.

One of the pitfalls of art as a spiritual discipline is that others often expect us to display our work or to share it with them in one way or another. Creations that come out of an inner listening are intensely personal. They are every bit as difficult to share as journal entries, personal prayers, or the content of meditation. The advantage of those other disciplines is that very few people expect them to be shared in a public way. To keep your artwork for yourself takes some strength.

There may also come a time when you are ready to share your creations, and this too presents questions. Choosing to share your creations requires you to be comfortable with the work and its place in your life, so comfortable that the responses of others do not change the meaning or the place of the work in your own life and practice. When you are at this point, then you can decide how and with whom to share your work. We must remember that creativity is about the process, not the outcome, especially when it is being used as a spiritual discipline. Creativity is about the experience, the identifying and releasing of feelings and core responses to the world around us.

I have found artwork to be a very powerful spiritual discipline, one that has allowed me to reconnect with parts of myself that I had long negated and devalued. Having integrated artwork back into my life, I feel a sense of wholeness that I had lost. I have also chosen to share my work through a public showing and found it to be a powerful affirmation of the balance in my life. That balance was brought about in large measure for me through the spiritual practice of creativity.

No matter what media or methods you explore, or how you choose to share your art with others, personal authenticity is the most important aspect of art as a spiritual practice. Listen to yourself. There are no limits. Use what you have, experiment, and eventually find what you like. This spiritual practice is based on tangible, tactile responses. If you do not feel in touch with the medium, if it in any way holds you back from self-expression, get rid of it and try something new. If you don't like painting on canvas, try painting on rocks. If pastels on paper don't work for you, see if crayons on fabric do.

The most important things are to find yourself and to let it out. Pay attention to your dreams and the inner workings of your mind and even to the colors you see. The more you pay attention to what you see and how you respond to it, the more material you will have for your creative endeavors. Artistic expression is from the soul, and no one else knows what yours contains, so let it out in your own way.

Resources

THE BASICS

For more information on the middle way, Michael A. Schuler recommends *Everyday Zen* by Charlotte Joko Beck (New York: HarperCollins, 1989); *Dakota* by Kathleen Norris (Boston: Houghton Mifflin, 1993); and *Wisdom Distilled from the Ordinary* by Joan Chittister (New York: HarperCollins, 1991).

ENGAGING THE MIND: Contemplation

To learn more about Zen, James Ishmael Ford recommends the various books by Robert Aitken, especially his classic *Taking the Path of Zen* (New York: North Point Press, 1982). Ford's book, *This Very Moment: A Brief Introduction to Buddhism and Zen for Unitarian Universalists* (Boston: Skinner House Books, 1996), is intended to directly address the questions of religious liberals who might be interested in Zen Buddhism.

For further information on Zen Mountain Monastery, Wayne B. Arnason suggests contacting Zen Mountain Monastery, PO Box 197, Mt. Tremper, NY 12457 (914-688-2228) to receive a program catalog, or checking their site on the World Wide Web at http://www.zen-mtn.org. Arnason also recommends the following introductions to Zen practice— *The Eight Gates of Zen,* by John Daido Loori (Mt. Tremper,

NY: Dharma Communications, 1992), and *Taking The Path of Zen,* by Robert Aitken (New York: North Point Press, 1982)—and the following general introduction to mindfulness meditation: *Wherever You Go, There You Are* by John Kabat-Zinn (New York: Hyperion, 1994).

For information on sacred reading, Susan J. Ritchie recommends *Discover Your Spiritual Type* by Corrine Ware (New York: Alban, 1995) and *Prayer and Temperament: Different Prayer Forms for Different Personality Types* by Chester Michael and Marie Norrisey (Charlottesville, Virginia: Open Door, 1984). Both of these works discuss several variations of the meditative component of sacred reading at length.

For further reading on the subject of silence and silent retreats, Andrew Kennedy suggests:

- *Sanctuaries, the Complete United States: A Guide to Lodgings in Monasteries, Abbeys, and Retreats* by Jack and Marcia Kelly (New York: Bell Tower, 1996).
- *Sharing Silence* by Gunilla Norris (New York: Bell Tower, 1993).
- *The World of Silence* by Max Picard, translated by Stanley Godman (Washington, DC: Regnery Gateway, 1988; originally published 1948).
- *Retreat* by Roger Housden (New York: HarperCollins, 1995).
- *Silence, Simplicity, and Solitude: A Guide for Spiritual Retreat* by David A. Cooper, which includes an excellent recommended reading list (New York: Bell Tower, 1994).

In Barbara Merritt's chapter, "Adversity," references to the story "Sheikh Kharraqani and His Wretched Wife" are from *The Essential Rumi,* translated by Coleman Barks with John Moyne (San Francisco: HarperSanFrancisco, 1995), pp. 219-220. Quotations from Rumi's *The Mathnawi* are from *The Mathnawi of Jalalu'ddin Rumi,* edited by Reynold A. Nicholson (London: Messrs. Luzac and Co.,

1925), Books V and VI. The poem "Absolutely Clear" is reprinted from *The Subject Tonight Is Love,* translated by Daniel Ladinsky (North Myrtle Beach, South Carolina: Pumpkin House Press, 1996), p. 50.

For more information on creating a home altar, Johanna Nichols notes that many sources of information about designing a center of spiritual focus come from earth-based traditions. Starhawk (Miriam Simos) has researched the ancient religion of the great goddess in *The Spiral Dance* (New York: Harper and Row, 1979). In the Native American tradition, read *Seven Arrows* by Hyemeyohsts Storm (New York: Ballantine, 1985) and *Buffalo Woman Comes Singing,* by Brooke Medicine Eagle (New York: Ballantine, 1991). In the Zen tradition, *Find a Quiet Corner* (New York: Warner Books, 1995) by Nancy O'Hara is helpful. If you want some guidance collecting rocks, Nichols suggests turning to Byrd Baylor's *Everybody Needs a Rock* (New York: Aladdin Books, 1987). You will probably find this in the children's section of your local book store.

If you are interested in learning more about Living by Heart, Laurel Hallman suggests consulting the video: *Living by Heart: A Guide to Devotional Practice,* with Harry Scholefield and Laurel Hallman (31 minutes). Available from *By Heart Video, L.P.,* 4347 W. Northwest Hwy, #120-293, Dallas, TX 75220 (toll-free 1-888-635-9999). Call or write to be put on a mailing list to receive information about further *By Heart* publications. If you are beginning to think about meditation and have never practiced on a regular basis, Hallman recommends *How to Meditate* by Lawrence LeShan (New York: Bantam Press, 1974). If you need a starting place to find poems to learn by heart, Hallman suggests considering the following:

- *Selected Poems of Rainer Maria Rilke,* translated and edited by Robert Bly (New York: Harper & Row, 1981).
- *House of Light,* poems by Mary Oliver (Boston: Beacon Press, 1990).

- *The Essential Rumi,* translated by Coleman Barks with John Moyne (San Francisco: HarperSanFrancisco, 1995).
- *Gitanjali* by Rabindranath Tagore (New York: Macmillan Co., 1913).
- *Life in the Forest* by Denise Levertov (New York: New Directions Books, 1975).

ENGAGING THE BODY: Activity and Nourishment

For more information on Integral Transformative Practice, Robert Hughes suggests consulting George Leonard's video, "The Tao of Practice," or *The Life We Are Given: A Long-Term Program for Realizing the Potential of Body, Mind, Heart and Soul* by George Leonard and Michael Murphy (New York: Putnam, 1995); or writing ITP at PO Box 609, Mill Valley, CA 94942. Hughes also recommends *The Future of the Body* by Michael Murphy. For information on Thomas Hanna's Somatic work, Hughes suggests reading Hanna's *Somatics: Reawakening the Mind's Control of Movement, Flexibility and Health* or writing to Somatics Educational Resources, 1516 Grant Avenue, Suite 220, Novato, CA 94945 for information about Hanna's cassette tapes.

ENGAGING THE HEART: Relationship

For further reading on everyday relationships as spiritual practice, Jane Ellen Mauldin suggests:

- Pema Chodron. *Start Where You Are* (Boston: Shambala Publications, 1994). With stories and suggestions from her Buddhist approach, Chodron sensitively and humorously guides the reader in a practice of developing greater awareness for the present day and moment.
- Laurie Abraham, et. al. *Reinventing Home: Six Working Women Look at Their Home Lives* (New York: Penguin Books, 1991). The authors' fascinating personal stories

help the reader assess the meanings we find in the small tasks and choices of our daily lives.

- Ronald S. Miller. *As Above So Below: Paths to Spiritual Renewal in Daily Life* (Los Angeles: Jeremy P. Tarcher, Inc., 1992). Tarcher's handbook addresses everyday spirituality for different people, including men, women, artists, and those healing from addictions.
- Scott Russell Sanders. *Staying Put: Making a Home in a Restless World* (Boston: Beacon Press, 1993). Scott's beautiful recollections of his own home place serve as a backdrop for his argument that claiming one place as physical and spiritual home serves to root us for everything we do in our lives.
- Rachel Naomi Remen. *Kitchen Table Wisdom* (New York: Riverhead Books, 1996). Remen's exquisitely sensitive stories, many about illness and healing, help the reader to examine his or her own life for the meanings that will help facilitate healing and spiritual growth.

For more information about marriage enrichment, M. Maureen Killoran suggests contacting the Association for Couples in Marriage Enrichment, Box 10596, 502 N. Broad Street, Winston Salem, NC 27108. The Benedictine prayer quoted in the chapter is found in John McQuiston II, *Always We Begin Again: The Benedictine Way of Living* (Harrisburg, Pennsylvania: Morehouse Publishing, 1996), p. 73.

ENGAGING THE WILL: Right Action

For more information on simple living, Ken Brown suggests contacting Seeds of Simplicity at PO Box 9955, Glendale, CA 91226, 818-247-4332.

For recipes and other information on a plant-based diet, Helena P. Chapin recommends:

- *Vegan Nutrition: Pure and Simple* by Michael Klaper, MD (1987, ISBN #0-9614248-7-7, Gentle World, Inc., PO Box

U, Paia, Maui, HI 96779). The book opens with a quote from Albert Schweitzer, "I am conscious that flesh eating is NOT in accordance with the finer feelings, and I abstain from it," and continues to discuss recipes, menus, nutrition, and the ethics involved.

- *Simply Vegan* by Debra Wasserman and Reed Mangels, PhD, RD (1991, ISBN #0-931411-05-XF1, Vegetarian Resource Group, Baltimore, MD 21203) is another useful resource about vitamins and minerals found in different foods, plus many delicious recipes.
- "EARTHSAVE, Healthy People, Healthy Planet" (706 Frederick Street, Santa Cruz, CA 95062-2205), an organization through which you may order the cookbooks above.
- *Vegetarian Times,* a magazine with many great vegan recipes.
- *Food for the Spirit, Vegetarianism and the World Religions* by Steven Rosen (1990, Bala/Entourage Books). In the preface, Isaac Bashevis Singer writes, "Vegetarianism is my religion. Rosen correctly points out that various philosophers and religious leaders have tried to convince their following that animals are nothing more than machines, put on earth for our pleasure, with no purpose of their own. Mr. Rosen smashes this idea."

ENGAGING THE SOUL: Creativity

To find *Art/Quilt Magazine,* Laurie Bushbaum suggests writing them at PO Box 630927, Houston, TX 77263-0927.

For more information on gardening as a spiritual practice, Barbara Davenport suggests:

- *Greening the Garden: A Guide to Sustainable Growing* by Dan Jason (Philadelphia: New Society Publishers, 1991). A lively practical guide to reclaiming control over the food we eat from a gardener in western British Columbia. Full of wise tips and useful advice for the novice or experienced organic gardener. An empowering challenge to the corporate control of food production and gardening. An enthusiastic celebration of the joys of gardening this good earth.

- *Growing Myself: A Spiritual Journey Through Gardening* by Judith Handelsman (New York: Penguin, 1996). Explores the healing power of inner gardening and deep levels of love and connection.
- *Planting Noah's Garden: Further Adventures in Backyard Ecology* by Sara Stein (Boston: Houghton Mifflin Co., 1997). A sequel to Ms. Stein's popular previous book, Noah's Garden.
- *People With Dirty Hands: The Passion for Gardening* by Robin Chotzinoff (San Diego: Harvest Books/Harcourt Brace & Company, 1996). A collection of both spiritual and humorous true stories of colorful, offbeat women and men whose passion is gardening and who are devoted to the promise of the earth.
- *Teaching Peace Through Gardening,* a children's gardening curriculum featuring gardening activities with cooperative games and art. Address: 4649 Sunnyside Ave., N. Room, Seattle, WA 98103. For information, call 206-633-0451.

For additional information on the spiritual practice of cooking, Lynn M. Brodie suggests:

- *Tomato Blessings and Radish Teachings: Recipes and Reflections* by Edward Espe Brown (New York: Riverhead Books, 1998).
- *The Enchanted Broccoli Forest* by Mollie Katzen, New Revised Edition (Berkeley, California: Ten Speed Press, 1995). In addition to many good recipes, this book also includes a section at the end (p. 273) that helps cooks learn how to improvise.

On artwork as a spiritual practice, Julie-Ann Silberman recommends:

- *Everyday Sacred* by Sue Bender (San Francisco: HarperSanFrancisco, 1997). In this book, Bender shares vignettes about creativity and the importance of paying attention to the self as we create.
- *The Artist's Way by Julia Cameron* (New York: Putnam, 1992). Focusing on creativity as a spiritual discipline, *The Artist's Way* is a particularly good resource for those whose creativity has been suppressed throughout their lives because it offers specific exercises to help in the process of unlocking the creative self.
- *Bird by Bird* by Anne Lamott (New York: Anchor Books, 1994) focuses on the methodology for creative expression. Lamott speaks about viewing things in manageable chunks, an important message in creativity of any sort.

About the Contributors

The Reverend Scott W. Alexander is senior minister of the River Road Unitarian Church in Bethesda, Maryland.

The Reverend Wayne B. Arnason is minister of the Thomas Jefferson Memorial Church, Unitarian Universalist, in Charlottesville, Virginia.

Jim Austin has practiced Vipassana (insight) meditation for about fifteen years and is a member of the First Parish Unitarian Universalist Church in Arlington, Massachusetts, where he occasionally teaches a course in mindfulness practice.

Lynn M. Brodie is preparing for the Unitarian Universalist parish ministry.

The Reverend Ken Brown serves the First Unitarian Universalist Church of Seattle in Des Moines, Washington.

The Reverend Laurie Bushbaum is a supply minister for the Unitarian Universalist Fellowship in Northfield, Minnesota.

Helena P. Chapin is minister of religious education at the First Unitarian Church in Rochester, New York.

The Reverend Barbara Davenport serves the Skagit Unitarian Universalist Fellowship in Mount Vernon, Washington, and is a campus minister at Western Washington University in Bellingham, Washington.

The Reverend Dr. Dorothy May Emerson, a Unitarian Universalist minister, is director of the Unitarian Universalist Women's Heritage Society.

The Reverend Marta Morris Flanagan is co-minister of the Unitarian Universalist Church in Portsmouth, New Hampshire.

The Reverend L. Annie Foerster is minister of St. John's Universalist Church in Cincinnati, Ohio.

The Reverend James Ishmael Ford is minister of the Valley Unitarian Universalist Church in Chandler, Arizona.

The Reverend Stephen H. Furrer is minister of East Suburban Unitarian Universalist Church in suburban Pittsburgh, Pennsylvania.

The Reverend Laurel Hallman is minister of the First Unitarian Church of Dallas in Dallas, Texas.

The Reverend Eva S. Hochgraf is assistant minister of the First Unitarian Universalist Church in Ann Arbor, Michigan.

Deborah Holder is a community organizer in Pittsburgh and, since 1993, has been executive director of Unitarian Universalists for a Just Economic Community.

The Reverend Robert T. Hughes is an extension minister at the Unitarian Universalist Church in Shenandoah, Virginia. He is also a licensed social worker and massage therapist.

The Reverend Dr. Andrew C. Kennedy is minister of the First Unitarian Society of Milwaukee, Wisconsin.

The Reverend Brian J. Kiely is minister of the Unitarian Church in Edmonton, Alberta, Canada.

The Reverend Dr. M. Maureen Killoran is minister of the Unitarian Universalist Church of Asheville in Asheville, North Carolina.

The Reverend Jennie Knoop is director of the Spirit Gate Retreat Center and chaplain at Triangle Hospice in North Carolina.

The Reverend Sarah Lammert is extension minister at the Unitarian Universalist Society of Ogden in Ogden, Utah.

The Reverend Dr. Tony Larsen is minister of the Olympia Brown Unitarian Universalist Church in Racine, Wisconsin.

The Reverend Edwin C. Lynn is minister of the Northshore Unitarian Universalist Church in Danvers, Massachusetts.

The Reverend Susan Manker-Seale is extension minister at the Unitarian Universalist Congregation of Northwest Tucson in Tucson, Arizona.

The Reverend Dr. Jane Ellen Mauldin is a Unitarian Universalist minister living in Covington, Louisiana.

Art McDonald, a former Dominican priest, has a PhD in Religious Studies from the University of Pittsburgh and is currently minister and director of social advocacy at the Allegheny Unitarian Universalist Church in Pittsburgh, Pennsylvania.

The Reverend Kathleen McTigue is minister of the Unitarian Society of New Haven in New Haven, Connecticut.

The Reverend Barbara Merritt is minister of the First Unitarian Church in Worcester, Massachusetts.

The Reverend Johanna Nichols is minister of the First Universalist Church in Auburn, Maine.

Dr. Rebecca Parker is president of the Starr King School for the Ministry in Berkeley, California.

The Reverend Aaron R. Payson is minister of the First Unitarian Universalist Society in Marietta, Ohio.

The Reverend Dr. Susan J. Ritchie is minister of the Dublin Unitarian Universalist Church in Dublin, Ohio.

The Reverend Dr. Michael A. Schuler is minister of the First Unitarian Society in Madison, Wisconsin.

The Reverend Julie-Ann Silberman is extension minister of the Unitarian Universalist Church in Kent, Ohio.

The Reverend Dr. Arvid Straube is senior minister of the Eno River Unitarian Universalist Fellowship in Durham, North Carolina.

The Reverend Dr. Audrey W. Vincent is minister of the Unitarian Universalist Church of Savannah, Georgia.

The Reverend Barbara Wells is minister of the Woodinville Unitarian Universalist Church in Woodinville, Washington.

Pat Westwater-Jong is a member of First Congregational Unitarian Church of Harvard, Massachusetts.

The Reverend Erik Walker Wikstrom is minister of the First Universalist Church of Yarmouth, Maine.